Crime & Criminals
OPPOSING VIEWPOINTS

OPPOSING VIEWPOINTS SERIES: Volume Thirteen

David L. Bender
Gary E. McCuen, Editors

GREENHAVEN PRESS, INC.
1611 POLK ST. N.E.
MINNEAPOLIS, MINNESOTA 55413

364
B

© 1977 by GREENHAVEN PRESS, INC.

ISBN 0-912616-20-2   Paper Edition
ISBN 0-912616-39-3   Library Edition

TABLE OF CONTENTS

TABLE OF EXERCISES

A major emphasis of this book is on critical thinking skills. Discussion exercises included after readings are not laborious writing assignments. They are included to stimulate class discussion and individual critical thinking.

INTRODUCTION

The purpose of this book, and the **Opposing Viewpoints Series** as a whole, is to present the reader with alternative points of view on complex and sensitive issues.

Perhaps the best way to inform oneself is to analyze the positions of those who are regarded as experts and well studied on the issues. Every reader will approach this book with some opinions of his own on the issues debated within it. However, the educated and well informed person should be able to recognize not only his arguments but those with whom he disagrees, for if one does not completely understand his opponent's point of view he really does not fully understand his own.

A pitfall to avoid in considering alternative points of view is to regard one's own point of view as being merely common sense and the most rational stance, and the point of view of others as being only opinion and naturally wrong. It may be that their opinion is correct and that yours is in error.

Another pitfall to avoid in seeking the best solution when considering controversial issues, is that of closing your mind to the opinions of those whose views differ from yours. The best way to approach a dialogue is to make your primary purpose that of understanding the mind and arguments of the other person and not that of enlightening him with your solutions and convincing him of their correctness.

It is the editors' hope that the reader of this book will enjoy a deeper understanding of the issues debated and will appreciate the complexity of even seemingly simple issues when good and honest men disagree. This awareness is particularly important in a democratic society such as ours, where men enter into public debate to determine the common good. People with whom you disagree should not be regarded as enemies, but rather as friends who suggest a different path to a common goal.

We would also like to caution the reader about being unwilling to take a stand on an issue because of a lack of information. That is an excuse and not a reason. One never has enough information. However, one should always be ready to form an opinion from the facts at hand. One should also remain flexible and be able to alter his opinion when new facts indicate that this is necessary.

CHAPTER

THE
CAUSES
OF CRIME

Poverty Is a Major Cause of Crime

Hubert Humphrey

Hubert H. Humphrey, a native of South Dakota, is currently a U.S. Senator from Minnesota. He was Vice President of the U.S. from 1965 until 1969 and early in his career he served as Mayor of Minneapolis. He is also an educator and author and has been a leading spokesman for Senate liberals.

Reflect on the following questions while you read:

1. Why does Senator Humphrey think crime is caused by poverty and unemployment?
2. What does the Senator mean by the term ''the new racism''?

Hubert H. Humphrey, **Congressional Record**, August 1, 1975.

We need only understand the lives of poor people to learn the cause and effect relationship of the criminal system and unemployment. Research reveals unmistakably that the majority of crimes of violence are perpetuated by males between the ages of 15 and 24 who are often unemployed or at the lowest end of the occupational and educational scale. You see, street crime, violent crime is essentially a problem of young and poor....

Unemployment and poverty are the tears of desperation in the young father's eyes when he cannot, no matter how hard he tries, provide enough food for the kids or some of the little pleasures for the family.

Unemployment may very well mean there is no longer any more health insurance, no decent health care. Fortunately we are going to take care of that in the Congress of the United States. It means there's no, or at least less, recreation — no cultural activity, no hope of becoming a productive, happy member of the community. Because the community has become a club of insiders. And the poor and the unemployed are the outsiders.

Yes, unemployment means much more than the loss of income. It means that society says, in effect: "We don't want you; we don't need you; and there is no place for you." Now, dear friends, that's not an economic fact. That's a social condition....

Sometimes we almost must get hit between the eyes with a social two-by-four before we will listen.

What happens when an offender is released from prison? Now I don't know enough about what goes on in the prisons, just what I've read. And what I've read is terrifying. I know this is one of the great problems that our legal system faces today, the prison system.

But just think what happens when a prisoner is released. We give an inmate $50 to $100 and a suit of clothes at the prison gate as he leaves. I ask you, how many hours could your household survive for $50 for rent and utilities, food and clothes? I think it's a self-answering question. And why should we expect $50 or $100 or $150 or $200 to last an ex-convict any longer?

Why should we expect it to last him for the four weeks it takes the typical ex-convict to come even close to finding a job?

The truth is, the criminals from whom we have the most to fear are not even a part of that statistical pool of 9.2% unemployed. They're the ones who have dropped off the bottom end. They have given up with the employment office. The unemployment rate is only a measure of the frustration they face in getting their lives together to become a constructive part of society. And getting it together means putting together the money to keep a family unit living together as well as getting together the self-esteem, the rebirth of pride and confidence that is the product of useful work.

Roy Justus, **Minneapolis Tribune**, September 11, 1968

4

I gather some of you may come to the conclusion that I believe in work. I do. I think it is constructive. It has therapeutic value second to none. It beats all the holding of hands and the consolation that you can give....

Violent and dangerous offenders must be separated from our society. But for many there are better ways. And they can be effective in steering the first offender away from learning the ways of crime and violence that we all fear.

The larger answer, however, lies in work, in jobs that are constructive, and particularly for the young.

I remember in the days of the Depression we had the Civilian Conservation Corps. Kids got in trouble then, too, you know. But they went to work. They did great things. I know that a government that wants to can do these things. I do not propose that we make every bank robber a bank teller or that we make every car thief a parking lot attendant.

But we can, and I say we must, assure every American that is willing to work, wants to work, has the ability to work, the right to earn his or her way with useful and, constructive and satisfying employment. Now that's the answer to a lot of our problems. And we get something out of it besides.

There's a whole nation to be re-built. We sit around here — we professional social workers — we sit around and wring our hands about the filth of the cities, the slums, the poor housing. We know it's there; we've recited it until we're blue in the face. In Washington, D.C., there is 14th Street, which was devastated as a result of the riots after the death of Dr. Martin Luther King in April of 1968. That was the trigger. Three Presidents have promised to clean up that section of town. We've re-built half the world in the meantime. But whole areas in Northwest and Northeast Washington were burned out and are not yet completely cleaned up. They stand there as a living testimonial to our indifference. I guarantee that if that had happened in Chevy Chase, where I used to live, if it had happened where middle-income people lived — if you don't mind me — it had happened where whites were living, they would have had it cleaned up. And you know it, and I know it.

5

Let me lay it on the line. The new racism is the neglect of the cities. Because it's there, where the old, the sick, the handicapped, and the minorities live. And that's why I intend to do everything within my power to arouse this Nation to a social consciousness as to what needs to be done. Not only to save our cities — that's not the only point — but to save our people. And the test of a good government is not only what it does for the majority but whether or not it metes out justices to the minority.

THE REAL CRIME

If we read closely into what is behind the crime statistics — poverty, lack of education, abysmal ignorance, lack of opportunity, lives lived in squalor, broken homes, broken lives — we read the future of the country. And that future is grim.

The United States is populated by a citizenry increasingly illiterate. This society is information rich, education poor. Information is at everyone's fingertips, but the education to do anything with that information is less and less available. Children deprived of education instead have their heads stuffed with nonsense and dangerous catch-phrases that seem to make sense.

We're a nation mind-deep in trash, emotional, moral and "educational" trash, the trash of "be happy" promises, the trash of cheap advertising, the trash of "get yours while the getting's good," the trash of the glossy magazine pages.

Education is not simply the adequate absorption of a given amount of information. It is the formation of a sense of values for oneself, a sense of service to society as a whole, a feeling of being obliged to consider the greater good.

What a contrast with the modern United States....

The United States has to look at its children and ask, "What do they need?" And we know the answer is guidance. They need smaller class sizes; they need models; they need people reaching into their minds and hearts with values — Judeo-Christian values, Buddhist values, humanitarian values, but values....

If there is a single goal for this society, it must be to educate our children, to expose all our children to values. If the taxes are to remove the second car from the family and eliminate the summer home, if a national health service is to be delayed, if the badly housed are to live yet more lives in squalor and disease, if the military is to go a thousand nuclear warheads short, it could all be justified if the sacrifices were made in the name of educating, truly educating, the children, the future....

Then we would be starting off toward a just society. And the criminal, too, would meet with justice along that way.

"The Real Crime," **National Catholic Reporter,** April 16, 1976.

The real moral test of government is what it does for those who are in the dawn of life, the children. For those who are in the shadows of life, the sick, the weak, the handicapped, and the needy. And those who are in the twilight of life, the elderly. Most everybody else can make it on their own. Those are the three areas where you test the moral stature or the moral fibre of a country and a government.

Yes, I am convinced that we can reduce crime. And I am convinced that we can reduce it at a price we can afford. But no amount of crime control can control crime in a major depression or recession, or while we have housing that is filthy and rotten, and neighborhoods that are disintegrating and communities that are falling apart. You can't do it under those conditions. You've got to get at the root cause. It doesn't solve all of the crime, of course. There are people who are murderers, rapists. There are people who are almost congenital burglars. That's another breed. But an awful lot of crime is committed by our young. Our people should be worried about the social environment in which we live, worried about the bigotry, the segregation, the discrimination, the intolerance, the ugliness, and the filth of the urban ghetto.

We cannot close our eyes to the terrible tragedy of human suffering and human neglect.

No, we cannot abandon our efforts to improve our police. I've worked a good deal of my life for that. Nor can we fail to provide the courts the means to administer justice promptly and fairly. We need that. We must insist that more resources be directed towards an efficient system of justice.

We cannot speak realistically about prison reform unless we are willing to make a strong and major investment in the improvement of our correctional facilities and in the training and the income of personnel at all levels who administer these correctional systems.

We cannot speak honestly and realistically about quickly apprehending criminals, solving crimes, or guaranteeing the right to a speedy and fair trial in the face of severely limited resources in our police departments, the public attorneys' offices and in our courts. When less than one-third of the crimes against property are solved by an arrest of a suspect, when in New York City two years ago the prosecutors had to deal with nearly 31,000 felony arrests — or 249 cases for each prosecutor each year — then it becomes sharply clear that our system of criminal justice is in urgent need of assistance just to cope with demands placed upon it, much less to undertake long over-due improvements and reforms.

But the heart of our victory will come from the determination to strike at the root of crime, as well as its symptoms. And surely the facts indicate that poverty, poor education, discrimination, lack of skills, and the ugliness of slums contribute to criminal behavior.

Therefore, we must launch an attack upon these sources of criminal behavior. And we must overcome

8

that poverty of spirit which destroys hope and breeds crime. The famous philosopher John Stuart Mill understood this challenge when he said, "Let a person have nothing to do for his country, and he will have no love for it."

The Myth That Poverty Causes Crime

Warren T. Brookes

Warren T. Brookes is a columnist for the **Boston Herald American**. He has also served as Research Director and Promotion Manager for the Christian Science Publishing Society. Mr. Brookes received his A.B. in Economics (Cum Laude) from Harvard in 1952.

Consider the following questions while reading:

1. What evidence does the author present to prove his claim that poverty does not cause crime?
2. What does Mr. Brookes think is the most fundamental cause of crime?

Warren T. Brookes, "The Myth That Poverty Causes Crime," **Boston Herald American**, 1976.

One of those "sociological myths" that doesn't seem to want to go away is that poverty causes crime — and that we won't reduce crime unless we first reduce poverty.

To the simplistic, the theory seems valid. Most people in prison are from a background of poverty — ergo, poverty must be the main cause of crime. Right? Wrong.

Because if that theory were literally true, crime would be decreasing in this country — instead of increasing, since poverty has been going down for 40 years or more. Unfortunately, for the theory's sake, as well as for the country's sake, exactly the opposite phenomenon has taken place.

The greatest *decline* in poverty has directly coincided with the greatest *rise* in crime in this nation's modern history!

The figures tell the story:

	Percent Living Below Poverty Line	Violent Crime Rate	Property Crime Rate
1950	27	167	1745
1975	12	434	3910
% Change	-55%	+160%	+124%

In short, in the period when poverty in this country declined by 55 per cent, violent crime *rose* by 160 per cent and property crime rose by 124 per cent.

Thus the argument that poverty causes crime is a statistical fraud. It won't wash in any way. The best proof of this lies not only in the statistics but in the more fundamental facts that:

• The lowest crime rates in this nation can be found in some of the most impoverished areas of the country.

• All 15 of the lowest-crime-rate-states in the U.S. are substantially *below* the U.S. median income.

Two of the nation's most impoverished ethnic communities are Chinese-Americans and Hasidic Jews — yet both have among the lowest crime rates in the nation.

• The nation's four highest-crime-rate cities: Ann Arbor, Mich., Fort Lauderdale, Fla., Phoenix, Ariz., and Las Vegas, Nev., are all ''rich'' communities with very low poverty populations.

Bender — **Waterloo Courier**

• The crime rate in many affluent suburban areas is now growing even faster than it is in most urban ghettos.

In short, the statistics clearly show that poverty has very little to do with crime, at least in so far as being a direct *cause* of crime.

• But don't take our word for it. This is the conclusion of a number of top university scholars working on the subject, including Prof. James Q. Wilson, of Harvard, Prof. Paul Ehrlich of the University of Chicago, and Prof. Gordon Tullock of Virginia Polytechnical Institute.

The work of these three men not only debunks the myth that poverty causes crime, but it shows that the most fundamental contributing cause to rising crime is quite simply declining punishment.

As Prof. Tullock sums it up, "There is no longer any question. Economists in the U.S., Canada, and England have shown conclusively that punishment does cut down on crime."

Prof. Ehrlich's studies of 50 U.S. states prove statistically that "states with better police protection, higher certainty of conviction and imprisonment, and longer prison sentences have lower crime rates than less permissive states."

He found that "society is now exacting a smaller and smaller price for crime. The conviction rate for burglary is less than half of what it was in 1960, for auto theft it has fallen by two-thirds, and for murder it has declined by 30 per cent."

What Prof. Ehrlich is confirming is the fact that contrary to many popular sociological myths, for the past 15 years fewer and fewer crimes have resulted in convictions and jncarceration, and prison populations have been declining relative to both the nation's population and the crime rate.

Nationally, between 1960 and 1970, there was a 139 per cent *increase* in crimes committed, and an 8 per cent *decline* in the country's prison population, which

RETURN TO
BASICS NEEDED

In my opinion one of the causes for the growing crime rate has been the decline of one of the basic tenets that this country was founded on — individual responsibility. Our forefathers believed that a person was responsible for his or her own actions. If a person did wrong, that individual should pay the price.

In recent years some sociologists and other social scientists have held that individuals are not responsible for their actions. Instead, individuals are supposedly products of their environment, the society, or various other forces. The result has been the decline of individual responsibility and at the same time a rise in crime.

Attempts to ignore facts of life have not negated those facts. They have not gone away. Human beings are responsible for their actions. A return to this basic view will help in deterring and punishing criminals.

Congressman John Ashbrook, "Return to Basics Needed to Fight Crime," **Human Events**, September 20, 1975.

means in simple terms that an offender stood a 62 per cent lower chance of going to jail for his crime in 1970 than he did 10 years before.

In Massachusetts, almost the same picture holds. Between 1960 and 1970, there was a 143 per cent increase in crimes committed, compared with only a 6 per cent increase in prison population — which translates into a 50 per cent drop in certainty of punishment in the Bay State.

Today, the average individual who commits a crime, including the repeat offender, in Massachusetts stands a 98 per cent chance of "succeeding;" that is, of avoiding any punishment at all. Less than 25 per cent of the state's repeat offenders have been going to jail, until recently.

All this may well be changing now, because under the direction of Atty. Gen. Bellotti, a more concerned effort is now being made to incarcerate the repeat offender — to ensure certain if not long punishment.

The statistics clearly show that this is the right direction to go. The figure also shows that the poverty-causes-crime myth should be buried forever.

Not only is this a fraudulent claim, but it only promotes more crime by giving people an excuse for ripping off the society in which they live. And the victims of this rip-off are invariably just as poor as the ones doing it.

A Businessman's View

John M. Burns

John M. Burns has been Vice President for Urban Affairs, Westinghouse Broadcasting Company, Inc., since 1969.

Use the following questions to assist you in your reading:

1. Why does the author think America will experience an increase in crime in the years to come?
2. The author calls our criminal justice a "non-system." What does he mean?
3. Why does the author think our present criminal justice system is a cause of crime?

John M. Burns, "Crime and Punishment in USA," **Fortune News**, August 1975, pp. 4-5.

For the past several years, I have attempted to keep in close personal touch with the criminal justice system in cities and also with those who break the law.

In my work, I meet regularly with judges, district attorneys, probation and parole officers, jail and prison officials, neighborhood youth workers, young street criminals, and inmates. I also ride full eight hour shifts with the police in high crime areas....

There is little doubt in my mind that crime in America is going to become much worse in the years to come. All the needed ingredients for an upsurge in crime are there: growing unemployment among our youth; the frustrated expectations of millions of young people, white and minority, who don't really believe that they will ever participate "legitimately" in the American dream; a long standing pattern of selective law enforcement in which certain classes of persons are singled out for inclusion in our exclusion out of the justice system; flagrant and growing disrespect for authority — in the home, the school and in the street.

And perhaps most disturbing of all, our modern street criminals and their white collar counterparts have learned that crime in America does pay and pay very handsomely — with a minimum chance of being apprehended, tried and convicted by a creaking, under-funded criminal justice system....

AT THE CROSSROADS

We are at the crossroads between repression and its doubtful results, and an intelligent handling of crime and its causes.... The answers will not come from seeing the crime problem as a police problem, but in seeing it basically as a citizen's problem. They will not be found if our police have to continue to serve as an occupation army in large segments of our great cities.

And answers will not come if we continue to allocate 75 to 80 percent of our criminal justice budgets to the police — leaving our courts, probation departments, and district attorneys to fight over the rest. And solu-tions to complicated questions will most certainly not be found if those who attempt to find them are kept on the defensive by those who cry "soft on crime" or "bleed-

17

ing hearts'' every time new ideas not involving force and repression are brought forth.

For those of us who look for answers beyond arms and might, it is not sympathy for criminals but regard for the preservation of order that dictates less emphasis on prison and massive police departments, and more on other proposals with long range potential for reducing crime....

A NON-SYSTEM OF CRIMINAL JUSTICE

And what do we have to meet this growing crisis? A criminal justice system that is not working within the context of our constitution. One that is just too swamped to deliver more than the roughest justice — and too ragged really to be called a system. What we have is a non-system in which the police don't catch the criminals, the courts don't try them and the prisons don't reform them. The system, in a word, is in deep trouble and Americans have only slowly awakened to the urgency of the matter.

Part of the trouble has been neglect — astonishing neglect of our criminal justice system. And the alarming rise in crime has made it painfully clear that neglect is a luxury the United States can no longer afford....

Where we have identifiable crime patterns, we cannot look for simplistic solutions. Black crime, youth crime, interethnic crime, white collar crime, organized crime are all products of our times. All have roots — substantial roots — in the patterns of neglect of the criminal justice system....

Many Americans take comfort in the view that crime is the vice of a handful of people. This view is, of course, inaccurate. The President's Commission on Law Enforcement tells us that in the United States today, one boy in six is referred to the juvenile court. Two million Americans are received in prisons or juvenile training schools, or placed on probation each year. The Commission also predicted that about 40 percent of all male children now living in the country will be arrested for non-traffic offenses during their lives....

18

CRIMINALS ARE MADE

Criminals are made, not born; criminals begin on the living room floor in front of the automatic babysitter called television; young crimnals are being trained by a generation of ''we don't care'' parents.

With the incredible breakup of American home life, the virtual disintegration and destruction of the most basic institution of all society — the family — already rampant crime steadily spirals upward. Children are far more likely to turn to crime if parents battle frequently, or if one or the other parent is missing, through divorce, death, or abandonment — or simply was never there in the first place because of illegitimacy.

Child abuse is also a factor. A child who is abused, beaten, and tortured is himself most likely going to become a brutal person. People tend to treat people the way they themselves have been treated.

Garner Ted Armstrong, ''Recycling Our Criminals,'' **Plain Truth**, September 1975.

This is truly a different generation of criminals — one that is very difficult, if not impossible, for authorities and others to reach. As a Boy's Club official in Boston put it: ''Father Flanagan would be hard pressed to communicate with our young white and minority street criminals and delinquents today.'' They are cynical. They live only for today. They think education is a rip off designed only for ''smart boys'' — not for the poor. They think everyone — the banker, the politician, the businessman — is into his own ''hustle'' — so why not us?

They don't want a job — most of them feel they couldn't afford the low wages. They believe that ''crime does pay, and pays very well'' — well enough for them to take their chances with the criminal justice system.

19

Milton Allen, State Attorney for Baltimore, told me that typical young criminals figure there is only a 10 percent chance of being caught — and they will risk much for these odds. Even if caught, they know their chances of doing time are quite slim, specially if they can afford a good attorney. And even if they go to jail or prison, Mr. Allen says, they "do time" better than any group of criminals he has seen over the past 30 years.

Allen and others are deeply concerned with selective law enforcement — which Allen characterizes as the nationwide practice by which certain classes of persons are singled out for inclusion in or exclusion out of the justice system. He doesn't believe we will ever make any substantial headway against crime unless and until we correct the abuses engendered by selective law enforcement.

More specifically, Allen describes the practice in these terms: "One form of selective law enforcement is failure to deal with interethnic crime in common sense fashion. This is the form where black on black crime, poor on poor crime is simply not investigated, prosecuted or judged properly. This is the form that gave rise or gives rise to the rule of thumb that 'a black man don't get no time for killing another black man' — with its sad legacy so evident today when black on black crime constitutes the bulk of all inner city crime.

This is the form that places different values on different lives, largely because of the personal feelings, prejudices and practices of the investigators, prosecutors and judges involved. The obvious result is the slackening of law enforcement as to interethnic crime because if we don't care about the highest of all crimes — murder — then certainly less serious interethnic crimes would receive even less attenion. So in every depressed area we have a burgeoning of interethnic crime that immediately forms a tighter and tighter vicious circle. Obviously, the easier it is to commit crimes, the more crimes will be committed; the more crimes committed, the harder they are to deal with; the harder they are to deal with, the easier they are to commit. Around and around it goes!...

Another type of negative selective law enforcement is practiced not because law enforcement does not care

THE PSYCHOLOGY
OF CRIME

In a series of articles Chicago Tribune reporters have tried to trace some of the causes behind Chicago's horrifying murder rate, which so far this year is averaging nearly four a day. Of all the facts and speculations brought out in their interviews, one stands out in our mind as the most chilling and perhaps significant.

It is that, for increasing numbers of our fellow citizens, life is unimportant. For them it seems to matter less than the chance of getting a few extra dollars, less than a spasm of anger or fear....

If we are to control this mindless murder, it is important to understand the psychology of those causing it. Some of the best clues, in our view, came from the reporters' talks with Otis Lee Thornton, 19, in prison for killing a man in a holdup.

Thornton does not see why he should be kept in prison for this crime. He said: "This man ain't coming back, even if they put me away for 300 years. I mean, why should a person be really punished for, you know, 'cause a human got killed?''

"Murder Becomes Mindless," **Minneapolis Tribune**, January 18, 1975.

but because they care so much. That is lack of enforcement in the area of white collar crime, official corruption and consumer fraud. Though adequate laws exist to protect the public from this type of criminal activity, we have barely scratched the surface in this area. The police have no attunement toward these types of crimes and very few prosecutors' offices are equipped to do the in-depth investigation needed to convict these offenders....

FINAL COMMENTS AND SUGGESTIONS

As I stated in my opening remarks, I believe we are at the crossroads in criminal justice. We must not shy away from reform, if we believe it to be good reform. We must not be afraid of those who would call us soft on crime, and we must effectively counteract the belief that there is a ''police solution'' to the crime problem. For in reality there is only a citizen solution to the crime problem. And it is citizen leadership groups that must find some hard answers to the problem — answers that go beyond the simplistic notion that if we buy more arms for the police and ourselves; if we lock up every offender for long periods of time; only then will we solve the problem.

No, we have to do more than that. Somehow we will have to find jobs for the 25,000 to 35,000 Philadelphia students who desperately need them. We have to allocate for the non-police criminal justice agencies more than their usual small piece of the budget. And we will have to monitor (perhaps with special truth squads) all those special interest groups (including the politicians and militants) who feed on our fear of crime, who sell us slogans like law and order, or black separatism.

We've had enough of all that. What we now need to do is to find answers — and especially answers to these questions: What is this system of justice that does its job so poorly, after all these years of trial and error? Who is responsible for the continuation of an ineffective, expensive, unjust and barbarous method of dealing with delinquency that produces only more delinquency? Where are our lawyers? They know how wretched it is. Where are our judges? They wrestle with its creaking machinery daily. Where are our scientists, who ought to be offering some remedies? And where, oh where, is the political and citizen leadership we so desperately need if we are to survive as a free and safe people?

22

VIEWPOINT 4

A Police Chief's View

Edward M. Davis

Mr. Davis has been Chief of Police of Los Angeles, Calif., since 1969. Chief Davis completed 34 years of service with the Police Department in September 1974. He is currently a vice president of the executive committee of the International Association of Chiefs of Police.

As you read try to answer the following questions:

1. What does Chief Davis mean when he uses the term sociopath?
2. What does Chief Davis think of community-based rehabilitative programs? Why does he think they contribute to crime?
3. What causes the great increase in crime we have experienced in America, in the opinion of Chief Davis?

Exclusive Interview with Edward M. Davis, "Tough Words on Crime by L.A. Police Chief," **Human Events**, March 22, 1975, p. 8.

Q. You were quoted in the paper the other day as saying that there were too many people who believed in Father Flanagan's philosophy, that there is no such thing as a bad boy. What did you mean by that?

A. Well, Father Flanagan, of course, did a wonderful job with runaway boys and his motto was that there's no such thing as a bad boy. As a young man I used to send money to Father Flanagan's Boys' Home. But a lot of people have been sold a bill of goods on the idea that there really is no such thing as a bad boy in terms of crime.

Psychiatrists — for as long as I've been a policeman, and that's 34 years — have told us that there is such a thing as a sociopath, described as a person who never developed a conscience, probably at a very early age when a conscience should have been developed.

And I remember the chief psychiatrist at San Quentin about 25 years ago making that statement to a large group of police officers and he described the sociopath, then called the psychopathic personality, as a person who has no conscience, a person who has an inability to postpone gratification. He said the sociopath is a person who is going to do what he wants to do, when he wants to do it, regardless of the consequences — nothing inhibits him. He is a rotten apple.

Now that was a man who had spent a lifetime analyzing convicts in San Quentin about 25 years ago. Two years ago, at an international symposium in Athens, we had people from all various phases of the criminal justice system, law professors and psychiatrists and police officers and prosecutors. We had a very distinguished panel of psychiatrists and I related the chief psychiatrist's story, and said that since so many years had passed, can psychiatric science today change a sociopath? Dr. Schmidt had said there's nothing that psychiatric science could do to change such a person, to build a conscience into him.

The answer of this panel of psychiatrists, each and every one of them agreed, and they were from all over the Western world, that there's nothing known today in psychiatric science that can develop a conscience into an adult that does not have a conscience. They point out that the conscience develops maybe in the first five or six years of life. This is a known fact in the behavioral sciences and yet our prison officials, our judges, over and over again, are expecting the impossible.

They find a very hardened and dangerous criminal and they turn him loose on society, and so I have referred to people who think you can readjust a dangerous criminal sociopath in society as "psychoceramics" — or crackpots.

"SOFT ON CRIME" ATTITUDE

Despite all the efforts of dedicated and conscientious local law enforcement officers, and despite large injections of Federal funds to assist them in crime detection and personnel training, violent crime continues steadily upwards. In most American cities, it is truly "America's most agonizing fact of life."

It ought to be self-evident that most crimes are committed by criminals, and that decent, law-abiding people have been betrayed by legal technicalities which have become loopholes in the law and strangled justice.

The U.S. Supreme Court decisions that have tied the hands of our local police are a major cause of the problem. The "soft on crime" attitude is also manifested in the new coed prisons, the rehabilitation concept that is such a dismal failure, and the parole-probation system that puts criminals back into society without any apparent concern for their past and prospective victims. About 80 percent of all felonies are committed by repeaters and only six percent of offenses result in imprisonment.

Phyllis Schlafly, "Crime and Punishment," **The Phyllis Schlafly Report,** March 1976.

I might just add that within the past 10 years we've been suffering in this country from a mild delusion having to do with rehabilitation in so-called community-based rehabilitation centers.

The philosophy goes something like this: prisons and correctional facilities have not rehabilitated. Therefore, we must not put people in them. Then they go on to say that the misbehavior occurred out in society and any successful adjustment can't be in an institution but must be in that society in which the person got into trouble; and, therefore, we will use community-based rehabilitative programs and put people back out into the society where they are under the care of a probation or parole officer.

This philosophy has been bought lock, stock and barrel by many judges. The sentencing practices in California courts deteriorated very greatly from sending dangerous sociopaths to the state prison to putting them out on the street on probation.

If we lump murderers, robbers and burglars together, 10 years ago we sent 36 per cent of them to state prison. Today, we send about one-half as many or about 16 per cent to state prison. So this demonstrates that the judiciary has bought the community-based rehabilitation concept to a very, very great extent.

Q. In what way has this contributed to crime?

A. What this adds up to in terms of crime is that in the year 1972, the latest year that I have complete figures for, that of the people who were convicted in Los Angeles County of homicide, 20.7 per cent of them were out on active parole and 11 per cent were on probation. So, 31.7 per cent of the homicides were committed by previously convicted felons free in our community.

In the crime of robbery, 27.5 per cent of the convicted robbers were on probation at the time they committed the new robbery, and 27.9 per cent of the convicted robbers were on parole at the time they committed the new robbery. That means that 55.4 per cent of all people convicted of robbery were on parole or probation at the time they committed this additional crime. And the figures on burglary are very similar.

26

"Open-Door Policy"

Now what this means is that we are in effect recycling dangerous criminals, through the police, through the courts, and back out onto the street without their being kept out of circulation. So of more than half of the very violent-type crimes and crimes that cause a great deal of fear, more than half the people that we have to deal with, are people we've already handled. People who if they had been kept out of circulation would not be victimizing additional citizens. Now this percentage was much less 10 years ago.

Now my theory is a very simple one. I believe that the nature of man is relatively immutable; that from one decade to another, even from one century to the other, there's murder and robbery and people who break into homes. What has happened to generate the great increase in crime isn't necessarily a higher percentage of dangerous anti-social people in society; it's a change in the way society has handled those dangerous persons. And so the police, in effect, feel like the little boy trying to empty the ocean with a sand bucket. As we pour the water up on the sand it runs right back into the ocean. We're recycling very dangerous criminals over and over again.

It's a Spiritual Matter

Donald D. Schroeder

Donald D. Schroeder is a senior writer for **The Plain Truth** magazine. Since 1959 he has worked as a news analyst in the Ambassador College News Bureau. He has written numerous articles on family problems, morality, and crime. He also writes and edits material for the World Tomorrow radio broadcast by Garner Ted Armstrong.

The following questions will help you to examine the reading:

1. What does the author claim is the most important cause of crime?
2. The author lists six major causes of crime. What are they?

Donald D. Schroeder, "Curing the Cancer of Crime," **The Plain Truth**, April 5, 1975, p. 9.

REAL CAUSES IGNORED

Various officials claim the causes of crime can be attributed to poverty, racial tensions, class struggle, drugs, alcohol, glamorization of crime, unequal justice, corrupt law enforcement, permissiveness, lack of parental guidance, or even diet and genetics. Most, maybe all of these reasons, have some degree of validity in some cases. Yet something *much bigger* is missing in modern criminal theory. Criminologists and crime fighters cannot put their finger on it because it is a *spiritual* matter.

Police, courts and penal institutions are failing to reduce the crime rate because they are almost totally dealing with *effects* — not causes. And most of them admit it!

Let's clearly define the *major* causes in our social fabric that are encouraging today's spiralling growth of criminal activity.

DECAY OF THE FAMILY

Standing as the primary defense against criminal influence is — or should be — the family unit. But parents by the droves, gripped with all the popularly promoted pressures of social acceptance, materialism and self-gratification have practically handed over their children to all the wrong influences. Instead of standing as a breakwater against the tide of permissiveness, the modern family unit too often is being swept away with it. No wonder we are experiencing a generation of youth and adults that have little respect for honesty, law, order, decency or principle.

Millions of modern homes, from poor to rich, are beset by the disease of permissiveness, erosion of high ideals, lack of right leadership, lack of self-discipline, honest character, warmth, love and stability. Nearly half of our nation's serious crimes are committed by teenagers. Much of this juvenile delinquency finds roots in wrong parental values, parental apathy, or other wrong influences.

Senator John McClellan who probed organized crime for 18 years, pinpointed this major failure: *"...I think you have to start in the home.* There seems to be a lack of proper respect and discipline in the home. And in the school there is certainly a great lack of discipline.''

UNDISCIPLINED EDUCATION

Once the homes have failed to develop an early consciousness of high moral values and right character, the modern school system can do little but hold *weak* reins on the resulting unpredictable student behavior. Too many schools merely concentrate undesirable youthful human behavior into one building. The school ground then becomes a huge transmission ground for criminal values and attitudes.

Many school administrations and teachers, sensing the desperate need to fill the huge moral and discipline gap, may attempt to discipline students, but they often end up cowed (or even terrorized) by bands of hostile students.

One recent editorial summed up modern education's moral deterioration: ''(The fact) that basic skills, good manners, moral standards and discipline have gone so far out of educational style as now to be termed ''alternative' is a measure of the depths to which public education has sunk.''

Schools do educate! But from too many of these morally emasculated schools, society is reaping little more than smarter criminals.

INEFFECTUAL RELIGION

The Ten Commandments, if kept in both letter and spirit, will deter crime.

One hundred thirty million Americans are church members. Forty percent attend church at least once a week. But it seems that you can't tell a churchgoer from a non-churchgoer in day-to-day business ethics or social relations. Why this mute influence of religion on modern values? The answer is, much of modern religious philosophy has been overcome by secular society's popular emphasis on a vague moral value system.

30

Much of modern religion has deteriorated into meaningless weekly (or semi-annual) ritual, to which the average churchgoer gives lukewarm lip service only for a variety of social reasons. For millions, materialism, pleasure seeking and the philosophy of "getting mine now" are idolized more than honesty, the fear of God, or respect for the Big Ten of Exodus 20.

The Word of God clearly states one ultimate deterrent to crime: "...by the fear of the Lord men depart from evil" (Proverbs 16:6).

The responsibility for failing to set forth powerfully the reality of God, his righteous laws, his ultimate judgment — as well as his mercy and forgiveness — lies at the door of the modern ministry.

PERMISSIVE SOCIETY

Movies, TV, advertisements, magazines and scandal sheets everywhere glamorize the violent, the lust provoking, or the perverse. Films now promote all kinds of racially oriented "criminal" hero-types as the virtual new idols and ideals of manhood (and even womanhood). The not-very-subtle message gets through to many youth: "crime and violence pay — money, status, sex — just be smart and don't get caught."

Crime pays all right. Whole areas of cities are virtual cesspools catering to the basest of human behavior. The public's furtive support of vice feeds a growing tyranny of organized crime. Everywhere youth are under pressure from their peers to conform to bizarre, criminal or unethical practices. Drugs and alcohol abuse plague all levels of society. Pornography, corruption high and low, dishonest business practices, corporate rip-offs, cheating, lying, stealing, ethnic and class prejudices, discrimination — you name it — all these plague our society and fuel our criminal or morally vacuous atmosphere. All the money or laws in the world won't put an end to them. They are due to wrong *moral* and *spiritual* values.

POVERTY

Popular criminal theory places great emphasis on

31

CRIME AND MORALITY

The link of law and morality is fundamental. The very inception of the nation and its political philosophy were rooted in the moral law as embodied in the Decalogue and the Sermon on the Mount. Surely these underlying moral principles have contributed to the country's astonishing growth and progress in 200 years.

Today, can it not be seen that the disintegration of morality in recent times — the obsession with materialism, the sexual permissiveness, the addiction to drugs, indecency, greed, dishonesty in business, and so on — have been accompanied by increased lawlessness in the streets? That the lowering of moral standards has destabilized families and left many young people rudderless and confused?

The great demand of the hour is to lift the moral tone of the nation. Encouragingly, this process of rejuvenation is already taking place as the scandals of Watergate have awakened moral sensitivities to wrongdoing in government, labor union, and corporate life. Hardly a day goes by without some exposure of illegal conduct and a new effort to improve laws and their enforcement. This, too, is an aspect of these morally turbulent times.

It is thus to be hoped that Americans not give in to a feeling of helplessness in the face of rampaging crime. They can even rise in indignation at this bald imposition on the peace and order of their lives. Above all, they can resolve to strengthen their own standards — in their personal lives, in their homes, in their public conduct — and foster that climate that will antidote criminal instincts and help keep them in check.

"Creating An Anticrime Climate," **Christian Science Monitor**, November 19, 1975.

poverty as a breeding ground for crime. And it is. Poverty concentrates the worst of human conditions, including criminal behavior. *But poverty is not an excuse for crime and violence,* as many seem to imply!

Bringing people out of poverty should be a major goal, but to suggest that poverty is an acceptable justification for crime and violence is an insult to the great mass of people of all races who have lived for years in deprived areas but who do not commit crime. Many poverty-stricken individuals — the greatest *victims* of violent crime — do not permit their condition to be an excuse for criminal behavior or disrespect for others.

CRIPPLED CRIMINAL JUSTICE

The surest way to promote a criminal society is to make sure crime pays. And tragically, in America, it pays frequently. Like almost every other institution, the U.S. criminal justice system has broken down, become seriously crippled and even blind.

Crime experts estimate of all reported major criminal offenses, only 7% lead to arrests, only 2% to convictions, only 1% to prisons, and none to the death penalty. The chance of being punished for a serious crime in the U.S. is only 1 in 100.

"Laws on books don't deter (crime)," says Senator McClellan. "It's the enforcement of those laws that is the deterrent."

But society's "thin blue line" of criminal defense, the police, find themselves in an unenviable position. Not only underarmed and overwhelmed by the staggering volume of crime they must deal with, law enforcement officials are often hamstrung by public attitudes and court decisions in their enforcement of laws.

Changing social values — particularly concerning the so-called victimless crimes — makes enforcement confusing and difficult. Many citizens scream for more police, but increased police population is no great deterrent to crime. Unfortunately, police corruption in some cities has seriously marred their image and undercut their much-needed public support.

Adding to the policeman's frustrations, today's courts, judges and lawyers are swamped with criminal cases — and a lot of liberal thinking. The result is much delayed justice, unfair justice, or no justice at all. Thousands of hardened criminals are released on the streets time and time again....

Our nation has violated one of the cardinal deterrents to crime: "Because sentence against an evil work is not executed speedily, therefore the heart of the sons of men is fully set in them to do evil" (Ecclesiastes 8:11).

Distinguishing Primary From Secondary Sources

A critical thinker must always question his various sources of information. Historians, for example, usually distinguish between **primary sources** (eyewitness accounts) and **secondary sources** (writings based on primary or eyewitness accounts, or other secondary sources.) A diary written by a Civil War veteran is one example of a primary source. In order to be a critical reader one must be able to recognize primary sources. However, this is not enough. Eyewitness accounts do not always provide accurate descriptions. Historians may find ten different eyewitness accounts of an event and all the accounts might interpret the event differently. Then they must decide which of these accounts provide the most objective and accurate interpretations.

Test your skill in evaluating sources by participating in the following exercise. Pretend you are living 2000 years in the future. Your teacher tells you to write an essay about the causes of crime in America between 1970 and 1980. Consider carefully each of the following

35

source descriptions. First, underline only those descriptions you think would serve as a primary source for your essay. Second, rank only the underlined or primary sources assigning the number (1) to the most objective and accurate primary source, number (2) to the next most accurate and so on until the ranking is finished. Then discuss and compare your evaluations with other class members.

Assume that all of the following sources deal with the causes of crime in America.

_____ 1. A speech in 1976 by U.S. Attorney General Edward Levi before a senate committee investigating crime

_____ 2. A biography written in 1992 by a convict, detailing his life of crime and prison experiences covering 30 years

_____ 3. The court transcript from the trial and conviction of a corporate executive found guilty of dishonest advertising in 1970

_____ 4. A book written by a juvenile probation officer in 1986 describing 20 years on the job

_____ 5. A senate speech in 1975 by Senator Barry Goldwater attacking crime

_____ 6. The annual FBI crime statistics for 1974, released in 1975

_____ 7. A British columnist writing about crime in America in a British newspaper in 1978

_____ 8. A Lutheran minister's sermon against crime in 1976

_____ 9. An essay by a criminologist written in 1996

_____ 10. A television panel discussion in 1987, involving prison wardens

_____ 11. A book on the causes of crime in urban societies, written by a Japanese sociologist in 1974

CHAPTER

DEALING WITH CRIMINALS

6

Punishment Prevents Crime

Fred E. Inbau and Frank G. Carrington

Fred E. Inbau is President of Americans for Effective Law Enforcement, Chicago, Illinois, a Professor of Law at Northwestern University, and the author of several casebooks and textbooks on criminal law and law enforcement.

Frank Carrington is the Executive Director of Americans for Effective Law Enforcement, Chicago, Illinois. He is a member of the bars of Ohio and Colorado.

Bring the following questions to your reading:

1. How do the authors define the term ''hard line'' approach to crime?
2. Who are most often the victims of crime?
3. The authors attribute the breakdown against lawlessness to three causes. What are they?
4. What do the authors think should be done to prevent crime?

The problem propounded by the topic of how to mount an effective crackdown on crime can be brought into perspective by considering two phenomena of the decade 1960 through 1969. They are: (a) during that ten year period, safeguards for the criminal accused and permissiveness toward lawless, violent acts reached heights in the United States such as no other nation has ever witnessed; and (b) in the same span of time, while our population increased by 13 percent, *serious crimes increased by 148 percent.*[1] The two are not coincidental. In any society, the incidence of lawlessness is directly related to the number of criminally inclined individuals who are at liberty to prey upon others, and it is precisely the permissiveness shown toward criminals in this country which has resulted in their being free to practice their depredations to an unprecedented extent.

Crime is caused by criminals; the fact is as simple as that. When a strongarm robber slugs his victim in order to relieve him of his watch and wallet, he has committed a crime. No amount of elaboration on the question of whether or not the assailant came from an environment of poverty or a broken home makes the robbery itself any the less a crime. Likewise, when a youthful demonstrator, intolerant of this country's pace in solving its social problems, throws a rock that strikes a policeman on the head, an aggravated assault has been committed. Apologists for criminal behavior may wring their hands as much as they like about the robber "striking out at a society which has brutalized him" or the demonstrator "merely expressing his idealistic young concern"; the fact remains that both are criminals.

THE HARD-LINE POSITION

The answer, then, to the question of how to mount an effective crackdown on crime lies basically in first recognizing that crime is committed by criminals, and second, in getting as many criminals as possible out of circulation so that they are no longer free to victimize the law-abiding.

---

[1] Based on the Uniform Crime Reports of the Federal Bureau of Investigation for the year 1969. Serious crimes are, for FBI reporting purposes, murder, rape, robbery, aggravated assault, larceny over $50, and auto theft.

This position is called the "hard line" on crime. It is not fashionable among certain liberal social scientists.
...

It is quite true that there is nothing particularly compassionate toward a law violator in advocating that he be locked up; yet it would seem that the worthy object of compassion would be the victim rather than the oppressor. If a 75-year-old woman on a ghetto street is knocked to the pavement because she has the temerity to struggle with a husky 18-year-old purse-snatcher — the result being a broken hip which, at her age, may never mend — the most elementary concepts of fairness would seem to dictate that the victimized woman is more deserving of our sympathy than her attacker.

When liberality dictates that the lawless remain free to victimize others, it is clearly misplaced. This, in short, is the hard-line position that we believe to be both realistic and valid; it favors consideration for the victims of crime and for public safety above that for the offender himself....

Just because we favor a hard-line approach, it does not mean that we are insensitive either to the factors in our society which breed criminals or to the tremendous importance of the rehabilitation of those who have been convicted and are amenable to rehabilitation. The breeding factors of crime — environmental, hereditary, educational, social, and economic — are, of course, elements which go into the making of a criminal. Anyone who is seriously concerned with the over-all problem, be he a hard-liner or not, must recognize the importance of these breeding factors, and he must also subscribe to the view that once a person has committed a crime every feasible effort should be made to re-habilitate him. But there is nothing incompatible between an acceptance of those two positions and a recognition of the need to make our society reasonably free from criminal harm — especially between now and the time when we are able to make effective progress toward those two general objectives....

THE CRIME PICTURE

The right to be safe from criminal harm — parti-

40

cularly among the poor and the racial minorities — has become an illusion. They are the ones who are most often the victims of crimes of violence — murder, rape, robbery, and aggravated assault....

JUSTICE NOT REVENGE

The purpose of criminal law is not to seek revenge, but to seek justice. The first object, in my own view, is not to deter, but to punish. Rehabilitation is all very well, but it misses the point. The primary idea is not to turn the criminal into a good citizen; the primary idea is to lock him up. Incarceration — plain and simple incarceration — has its merits....

Here in Washington, police are searching for a 34-year-old man charged with running a tremendous heroin operation. The man is accused of corrupting and recruiting teen-agers, turning them into addicts and peddlers.

Assume, for the moment, that the suspect is arrested, indicted, fairly tried with every protection of due process of law, and found guilty. What then? I would hang him from a gallows in the nearest public square or, that failing, lock him up for life. This would destroy him? Let me dry my eyes....

Our system of criminal justice must be revitalized with a view toward punishment that is quick and effective.

James J. Kilpatrick, "Crime Must Be Punished," **Minneapolis Star**, April 7, 1975.

More dramatic than statistics on crime is the manner in which the lives of all of us, particularly the poor and members of minority groups, have had to be adjusted because of the ever-present threat of violent crime. In most of our cities, the law-abiding citizens have had to surrender possession of the streets after dark to the robber and those who may even bludgeon someone out of sheer delight. Many persons are literally afraid to leave the sanctuary of their homes for fear that they will fall victim to some form of violent attack; and for those who must be out on the streets, protective measures, unheard of ten years ago, are being used. Taxicab drivers, for example, no longer favor their passengers with opinions because the customer cannot hear the driver through the two-inch thickness of bullet-proof glass which separates the front and rear seats of most taxicabs today. Bus riders must prepare themselves with the exact amount of their fares because, nowadays, bus drivers do not carry change in order to discourage robberies. In short, we have been forced to accommodate our lives to the spectre of criminal terror....

WHY WE ARE NOT SAFE

Why is our crime picture as horrendous as it is, despite overwhelming public opinion against lawlessness? The answer lies in the fact that in many — far too many — cases, the law enforcement processes in this country have broken down, with the result that more and more criminals are free to prey upon the law-abiding. This breakdown is threefold, and stems from:

1. Failure to apprehend criminals
2. Failure to convict criminals
3. Failure to incarcerate criminals

When we analyze each of these failures, it becomes apparent why we are not safe and why a hard line is needed.

Failure to Apprehend

The deficiency of failure to apprehend in our criminal justice system is related to the law-enforcement function, but this in no wise means that it is the fault of our police departments.... One reason for this is the shortage of policemen, particularly in the core cities where they are needed most....

Another reason for underpolicing in some areas of

42

large cities is the understandable reluctance of police officers to subject themselves to the risk of assassination while on patrol....

All police officers accept the risk of being killed in the prevention of serious crime and in the course of apprehending criminals, but it is asking too much of them to incur the increasing risk of an assassin's bullet.

Police are also becoming more reluctant to make arrests at the scene of a crime or disturbance out of fear that they will perhaps attract a crowd and touch off a riot, or for fear that an arrest of certain individuals or groups of individuals will result in allegations of "police brutality" or other false charges.

Court-imposed restrictions of an unrealistic nature — which in our opinion were not constitutionally or practically required — serve to further inhibit the conscientious police officer: for instance, the Miranda rule[2] requiring a litany of advice about legal rights before the interrogation of an apprehended suspect can be conducted.

Failure to Convict

Even if a criminal is arrested, the likelihood is great that he will not be convicted. According to Senator John L. McClellan of Arkansas, in recent years verdicts of not guilty in robbery cases have increased 23 percent, and in burglary cases 53 percent.[3] The hedge of procedural safeguards which the Warren Court erected around the person accused of a criminal offense and the efforts of the judiciary to "police the police" have created such a maze of technical requirements for police conduct that, in case after case, obviously guilty persons must be freed because an officer neglected to act with the propriety demanded by the Court. Senator McClellan has characterized this situation as one in which the Court's rulings have threatened "to alter the nature of the criminal trial from a test of the defendant's guilt or innocence to an inquiry into the propriety of the policeman's conduct."[4]

[2] **Mirandva v. Arizona**, 384 U.S. 436 (1966).
[3] 115 Congressional Record 59565 (July ed., August 11, 1969).
[4] Ibid.

At the core of the barrier which has been erected between the factual guilt of a person and the legal proof of guilt is the so-called "exclusionary rule." This rule, which was made a part of the jurisprudence of this nation by a Supreme Court in 1961,[5] holds that no evidence, regardless of how relevant or probative it may be, can be used against a defendant if it was improperly obtained. For instance, if a dope pusher has been found in possession of narcotics but the search of his person, automobile, or room which revealed the narcotics is held to have been illegal *for any reason*, the narcotics cannot be used as evidence against him. Thus, the upshot of the exclusionary rule is that the *question of actual guilt or innocence is completely disregarded;* if the policeman has blundered in the slightest, the guilty party must be released — returned to society, free to continue his career of crime....

Failure to Incarcerate

On one recent day in Chicago — identified in a local newspaper editorial as a red-letter day for convicted criminals — the following events occurred:

• A sixteen-year-old killer of another teenager was found guilty of murder. He was placed on probation for five years because it was his "first offense."

• A seventeen-year-old pleaded guilty to setting fire to a police car, striking a policeman, throwing rocks and bottles at policemen, and grabbing a policeman's gun while resisting arrest. He, too, received probation. This was his "first offense."

• Three Black Panthers pleaded guilty to buying machine guns and hand grenades for the party's arsenal. Each one was given three years' probation, even though two of them had been fugitives and one had been convicted of assault and battery growing out of the shooting of a policeman.

These cases are illustrative of one of the reasons why the streets are no longer safe....

5 **Mapp v. Ohio**, 367 U.S. 643.

TIME TO USE THE BIG STICK!

Courtesy of the **Anoka County Union**

WHAT CAN BE DONE?

The answer to what can be done lies, in our opinion, in a massive outpouring of active citizen concern and involvement....

1. In the area of failure to apprehend criminals, there must be massive citizen support for the policeman when he is doing his job properly. This will create a

45

climate under which police recruiting will be enhanced and officers will not hesitate to do their job for fear of civil suits by vocal pressure groups such as the American Civil Liberties Union and other "police watcher" organizations....

2. In the area of failure to convict criminals, public outcry and pressure are necessary to curtail drastically those contrived "rights" of criminal suspects which serve only to protect the guilty without any compensating benefits. This can be done without diminishing the basic rights of all citizens. For instance, the Fourth Amendment's guarantee of freedom from unreasonable search and seizure must be preserved, but it can be done without the use of an exclusionary rule that turns so many guilty persons loose; moreover, it is ineffectual, anyway, as a police disciplinary measure.

The exclusionary rule should be removed from our criminal justice system and replaced by procedures for dealing directly with the officer who willfully violates a person's constitutional rights. Great Britain has never had the automatic exclusionary rule as we know it, and that country has never been turned into a police state.

3. In the area of failure to incarcerate, there are those who believe that the sentencing process is nobody's business but the judge's. This is not true. It is the function of a judge to sentence a convicted criminal; but the sentence itself — the determination of whether, or how soon, a potentially dangerous felon will be released into the community — is clearly the business of the community whose safety is involved. Just as the President, a governor, or a state or national legislator is accountable to the people in the final analysis, so is a judge whether elected directly or appointed by elected officials. In this area, citizen concern can be translated into action, as has been done already in several jurisdictions, by citizens' groups who follow a judge's sentencing record and then report, pro or con, to their fellow citizens.

CONCLUSION

Our suggested solutions to the crime problem are admittedly "hard line," but we believe that such an approach must be taken. If crime is to be significantly diminished, the concern of the law-abiding citizen will have to be translated into constructive action. Lawlessness threatens to engulf this country, and a firm stand is necessary to stem the tide.

Alternatives to Punishment

Judge Charles R. Richey

> The following speech was delivered by U.S. District Court Judge Charles R. Richey, to the assembly at the Conference on Alternatives to Incarceration, sponsored by the National Task Force on Higher Education and Criminal Justice and the National Council of Churches.

Reflect on the following questions while you read:

1. What reasons does the author cite for recidivists, exoffenders committing new crimes?
2. What alternatives to punishing criminals does Judge Richey suggest?
3. Judge Richey doubts that imprisonment deters criminals, with one exception. What is that exception?
4. What lesson does the author think we could learn from our early American forefathers regarding criminals? Do you agree?

Charles H. Richey, ''Judge Richey's Unique Perspective,'' **Fortune News**, November, 1975, pp. 7-8.

PUNISHMENT IS THE ONLY JUSTIFICATION FOR PRISONS

The only justification to me for incarceration in a penal institution today is *punishment.* Whether the certainty of punishment is a *deterrent* is really an unanswered question which needs a lot of further study by the behavioral scientists and others who are more expert in the field than Judges.

Before proceeding to the main subject-matter of my talk today, I want to emphasize the fact that whatever people say about the desirability of more punishment in the form of longer sentences in penitentiaries we should all remember that 97% of those presently incarcerated will someday be back in society again. If you will just examine the record, you will find that most ex-offenders will become recidivists and probably engage in more sophisticated and vicious criminal conduct than before — all as a major result of their incarceration in the first place. There are many reasons for this but *some* of the principal ones are as follows:

1. Inadequate provision and properly trained staff for realistic educational and vocational opportunities outside our closed institutions;
2. Lack of properly trained staff for treatment of emotional, mental, and physical disorders;
3. Insufficient training by properly trained and sensitized staff for counselling as to appropriate goals and how to achieve them outside a closed institutional setting;
4. The myriad of discriminatory laws on our city, county, state and federal levels which prevent ex-offenders from securing meaningful employment;
5. The lack of a properly trained staff of guards operating within our closed institutions who maintain daily control over our offenders;
6. Our insensitive, knee-jerk, and antiquated parole system which is presently heading in the direction of holding people within institutions based solely on the ''severity of the offense,'' whatever that means;
7. A monotonous and inadequate diet;

49

8. Lack of access to adequate libraries; and
9. Lack of access to family and friends in the outside world during incarceration; and
10. Lack of elemental safety from murder, rape, and other heinous crimes against inmates while incarcerated.

This list could go on and on but I give these only as examples of some of the things that need to be changed lest we make our offenders even worse than they generally are upon their release....

REHABILITATION THAT WORKS

The only place where "rehabilitation" in a meaningful and realistic sense can truly take place for all but about 15% of our offenders is in what has come to be known as *Community Treatment Centers* or *Half-Way Houses*. A major problem there, however, is not only lack of adequate funding, but their location in various communities across the country. Everyone says it is fine to have this, but don't put it near my house — put it in someone else's neighborhood.

The state that seems to have gone the furthest in the direction of abandonment of our old system to the relatively new concept of community-based corrections is Minnesota. Like Norman Carlson at the federal level, they candidly admit that they don't know how to achieve "rehabilitation." They say they have a higher priority, and that is justice. In the February, 1975, *Corrections Magazine*, the Minnesota Corrections Department mission is stated as follows:

> Justice is the central virtue for all public institutions and programs. Every person is entitled to the most extensive basic liberty to the degree that it does not violate and is compatible with like liberty for others. It follows that, with few exceptions, curtailment of freedom should be limited to the degree of control necessary for the protection of others from the offender. Control beyond the degree necessary for this purpose is a violation of the offender's rights.

I agree with that statement. Also, you should know that Minnesota prisons are about half empty because of their commitment to the concept of community-based corrections.

WE CAN DO MORE

Those of us who advocate prison reform and rehabilitation programs do so not out of a sense of charity, but out of a knowledge that bad prisons make bad prisoners worse human beings. The antireform advocates have received generous media coverage in part because the public mood demands that something be done about the nation's appalling crime rate. Sensing the public mood, most politicians understand too well what former Louisiana governor Earl Long said upon opposing an attempt at prison reform: "They ain't no votes in prison."

Considering the modest sums currently spent on rehabilitation programs it's odd that the government is making such a fuss about it. The cost of all forms of federal, state, and local rehabilitation amounts to less than five percent of the $5 billion spent annually on prison operations and construction. In general, the U.S. spends less than $100 per inmate per year for recreation, religion, social work, medical care, psychotherapy, counseling, education, job training, and placement for the more than two million men, women, and youths who pass through the country's prisons each year.

Surely we can do more.

Sol Chaneles, "Prisoners Can Be Rehabilitated — Now," **Psychology Today**, October 1976, p. 134.

Minnesota has another idea worth mentioning, and that is their new program which began in August, 1972, called the *Restitution Center Program*. After about four months in prison, candidates are screened for release to the program, upon their agreement to enter into a signed contract whereby the offender agrees to pay back the victim of his robbery or burglary, and is given help in finding employment and also allowed to visit with his family on weekends and certain weekday evenings as he earns such privileges. He is also given a wide variety of treatment alternatives which is divided into four phases, whose standards he or she must satisfy before the offender is placed on parole with little or no supervision. My friends, I must tell you that this program is not without its shortcomings, but it has, on balance, worked and, in my opinion, points out for us an alternative to what we are doing in most of the country at great cost to the public today. I commend it to you for further investigation and thought.

A similar community program has been established in Saginaw, Michigan, and early results are that only 2.5% of repeat offenders who were assigned to that project rather than being sent to prison were terminated because of new violations. This is a great deal less than the national recidivism rate of 60%, and the program is being operated at *one-fifth* of the cost of maintaining those same individuals in a prison setting.

And now, back to whether jail is a *deterrent*. I said earlier I have grave doubts that most offenders are really deterred by the possibility of incarceration. There is at least one exception, and that is in the area of white-collar crime. This should be pursued by all elements of the criminal justice system vigorously. However, again I must add this question. Aren't we innovative and civilized enough to punish white collar offenders in a manner that will deter others without putting a man or woman in jail to stagnate and perhaps be literally killed? I would suggest that compulsory public service with maximum supervision and loss of everyday freedom for white collar offenders could be a great resource for our disadvantaged and oppressed citizens. Why not take a doctor or businessman who cheats on his income tax and put him in the ghetto for a period of time instead of jail to live and work to serve the needs of the people there, instead of in prison? This is just one example and you can think of many more.

Before we do this, however, we have got to make another commitment, and that is not to keep our jails just for the unskilled and poor. They have potential, too, but we must train and educate them and lead them into a more productive and full life if there is to be equal justice under the law. This can be done at less cost and more public benefit in the long run out of prison than within if the business and professional communities will join together in setting up jobs and training programs for these unfortunate people. I tell you it can be done, and where there is a will, there is a way.

As to jail solely for punishment, I am very uncertain as to its real viability. Sure, there must be punishment for our offenders, but again I would say that this can take many forms and it depends, for its effectiveness, on each individual who is different and that person has the right to be considered on his or her own merits and possible danger to society. This is a delicate balance which we Judges are called upon to make all too frequently these days. I just hope we can somehow find a better way than our present system of a single Judge determining a man's loss of liberty without some element of review....

Prisons are destructive to prisoners and those charged with holding them.

Confinement is necessary only for offenders who, if not confined, would be a serious danger to the public.

For all others, who are not dangerous and who constitute the great majority of offenders, the sentence of choice should be one or another of the wide variety of noninstitutional dispositions.

The Nondangerous Offender Should Not Be Imprisoned, a policy statement by the National Council on Crime and Delinquency, May 1, 1973, p. 449.

In summary, let me repeat the following:

1. Our entire correctional apparatus is in need of drastic surgery with new emphasis on the need for community treatment centers for our criminal law offenders;
2. We should work to eliminate our present antiquated penitentiaries for all but about 15% of our offenders and give the remaining 85% vocational training, counseling

53

and therapy, and jobs in a community treatment center or halfway house setting;

3. Let us work to eliminate our discriminatory laws which prohibit our ex-offenders from gaining meaningful employment and thus a useful life as taxpayers;

4. Let us not panic when we hear the law and order people scream about the need for new and larger penitentiaries, or when they demand longer sentences and particularly the mandatory minimum type based solely on the offense;

5. Let us study to make the life of those in prison at least decent and humane, and when they get out let us also make sure we have programs available to help them re-establish their lives as full-fledged citizens;

6. Last, but not least, let us abandon the notion that prisons can rehabilitate people as they are presently constituted and operated. When we realize this, the notion that long jail sentences will solve our crime problem will no longer be viable even to the unsophisticated and untrained observer of our public affairs....

In conclusion, I am reminded of the body of principles of justice for America which were written by the Quakers and such civic leaders as Benjamin Franklin, Benjamin Rush, and William Bradford in the early beginnings of our country. I submit that we have digressed a long way from these lofty ideals and that they offer much for us to consider seriously today:

"Our obligations are not cancelled by the crimes of the guilty."

"We must extend compassion to the guilty."

"The links for binding the human family together must under all circumstances be preserved unbroken — there must be no criminal class."

"Such punishments may be devised as will restore them to virtue and happiness."

VIEWPOINT

Justice Demands Punishment: A Christian Response

Lawrence J. Crabb, Jr.

Dr. Crabb holds a Ph.D. in Clinical Psychology from the University of Illinois. Once Director of the Psychological Counseling Center at Florida Atlantic University, Florida, he is now in private practice in Boca Raton.

Think about the following questions while you read:

1. Why does the author think that a truly humanitarian and Christian way to deal with lawbreakers is to punish them?
2. What does the author think is wrong with the treatment model of dealing with criminals?

Excerpts from "Should Lawbreakers Be Treated or Punished?" by Lawrence J. Crabb, Jr., reprinted by permission from the **Journal of the American Scientific Affiliation 28**, 66, June (1976). Copyright by American Scientific Affiliation, 5 Douglas Ave., Elgin, Illinois 60120.

C. S. Lewis once wrote that Christians must oppose the humanitarian theory of punishment, root and branch, wherever they encounter it. The view which Lewis so strongly rejected does away with the idea of punishing moral wrong and replaces it with the more "humanitarian" purpose of rehabilitating social deviants by psychological treatment....

CONTRADICTIONS BETWEEN THE BIBLE AND THE TREATMENT MODEL

The most serious objection to the humanitarian theory of punishment is theological. Christians believe that there really is a personal God, with a definite and revealed character. Any system of thinking must be ultimately measured by whether it can be gracefully integrated with what the Bible says about the character of God. The really frightening danger is that some people think that the treatment model for prisons which utterly disregards questions of morality is wonderfully consistent with Jesus' emphasis on peace, love, acceptance, forgiveness, and restoration. One seldom hears great terms like truth, righteousness, holiness, and justice. And yet Jesus' primary purpose in coming to earth was to satisfy the claims of a holy and just God against our unrighteousness. An approach to discipline (whether in society or in the home) which teaches that we must appeal only to the good in people, show them their wrong, set a good example, and positively reward desired behavior assumes that if God is there at all, He is not offended by moral wrong but is patiently indulgent in a grandfatherly sort of way.

Skinner teaches that you should not punish, only reinforce. Adlerians tell us that punishment is never appropriate. Deal with misbehavior by letting the offender experience the consequences of his own behavior. When he sees the rationality behind right living, he will evidence his inner goodness and intelligence by shaping up. The problem with such thinking is that it consistently misses the entire Biblical teaching about sin. Menninger's book **Whatever Became of Sin** hints in the right direction but falls woefully short of providing a substantive definition of sin based on an understanding of God's character. For Menninger, sin is social offence. For the Christian, sin is a culpable, punishable, heinous offense against a holy God. Man is not good, he is bad. While he may be able to see rational reasons for limiting self-indulgence, he basically does not want to change and is truly incapable of really changing. If the Bible is correct in its presuppositions about people, dealing with lawbreakers by building up their individualistic self-expression and letting loose an assumed positive nature will not really work in the long run, nor is it doing the criminal any favor. This last point needs to be underlined. A truly humanitarian approach to dealing with lawbreakers is to fairly punish them. They need to experience the sternness of the law. Paul says that God's inflexible commandments are intended to function like a schoolmaster to bring us to Christ by pointing up our helpless inability to ever satisfy a holy God. The treatment model takes all the sting from the law and renders impotent a God-ordained instrument for driving people to Christ.

> **We need to return to the Biblical position that criminal, delinquent, and immoral behavior is the expression of man's sinful nature and is not to be taken merely as evidence of psychological maladjustment.**

The treatment model for dealing with moral wrong implicitly denies the central act of all history. Christ's atonement for our sin. His death is reduced to merely a wonderful example of forgiving those who despitefully use you. According to this view, Jesus knew that those who killed him were misguided people who simply did not understand. His words of forgiveness are held up as a model for dealing with lawbreakers. The fact that Jesus could offer them forgiveness only because He was at that moment enduring the punishment from a righteously angry God which their sins (and my sins) deserved, is not recognized or believed.

The kind of individualism which encourages people to concern themselves with being true only to themselves not only goes against Biblical teaching like "esteem others greater than ourselves," "submit one to another," "bear each other's burdens," it also denies validity to any external authority before which one must bow. We need to return to the Biblical position that criminal, delinquent, and immoral behavior is the expression of man's sinful nature and is *not* to be taken merely as evidence of psychological maladjustment. It must therefore be firmly and primarily dealt with according to God's standards of holiness and justice and *not* according to man's psychological theories of treatment. Government is ordained of God to enforce the law responsibly in order to keep sinful man from totally destroying himself. Those who break the law have committed a real moral offense and deserve punishment. People are responsible and morally culpable for criminal behavior. Lawbreakers must not be regarded primarily as non-responsible, emotionally disturbed people in need of therapeutic assistance. Efforts to rehabilitate through counseling are right and proper but must never replace righteous and just discipline. Counseling is helpful and appropriate when it fits within the concept of justice and moral responsibility and when it recognizes that the fundamental problem with people is spiritual. Only regeneration provides a real and lasting answer. Any other approach denies the character of God and must be "...opposed root and branch wherever we encounter it."

Forgiveness, Not Justice: A Christian Response

Sister Dorothy H. Donnelly, CSJ

Sister Dorothy Donnelly is an associate professor of the Pacific School of Religion, Graduate Theological Union, Berkeley, California. She has published in the **New Catholic Encyclopedia**, the **National Catholic Reporter**, **Commonweal**, **New Catholic World** and books on human communication and pastoral spirituality.

Consider the following questions while reading:

1. Why does Sister Dorothy claim prisons ''do not heal, correct, grow human beings according to Judeo-Christian values''?
2. How does she respond to the question ''Am I my brother's keeper?''
3. What does she think is necessary for rehabilitation to succeed? Do you agree?

Sister Dorothy H. Donnelly, CSJ, ''Forgiveness, Not Justice: A Christian Response,'' **National Catholic Reporter**, October 1, 1976, pp. 5, 10-11. This article is excerpted from her forthcoming book **Jackets**.

Is incarceration justified?

By what principles do we have the right to take five, 10 or 20 years of another person's life? In the existing system a prison sentence is a life sentence because of the hardness of our hearts which will not forgive the offense, although we beg God for forgiveness in the Lord's Prayer and, incredibly, ask to be forgiven *according* to the measure that we forgive others.

What right do we have to make scapegoats (and prisoners) of the poor, the uneducated, the minority persons whose conditions move them routinely toward prison?

What and who is a criminal and by what criteria?

What is the basis of the belief that criminals must be punished?

Lastly, how can we possibly assume human beings can know the precise degree of another's moral guilt and actually set an amount of personal suffering to compensate for the harm they've caused? The more we discover about humanity, about consciousness, about the effects of environment, education, culture, the more we know that we know very little, and surely not enough to make the tremendous value judgments implied in the taking of 10 years or the life of another.

Jesus preached kindness and forbearance toward even the enemy. The Jewish principle of *chesed* or steadfast love binds the entire community, while the Talmud insists upon the need for special care for the poor, the uneducated, the offender.

Jesus so lovingly combined the Old and New Testament by reading from Isaiah: "The spirit of the Lord is upon me because he has anointed me; he has sent me to announce good news to the poor, to proclaim release for prisoners...to let the broken victims go free.

It is fascinating to see Jesus, here as the prophet of the New Testament, speak out for God; hatred, warfare, inhumanity, cruelty, and the death we create among ourselves must end. "Freedom to the prisoner" is the first notice about the meaning of what he calls reconciliation.

THE REAL ISSUE

The real issue is not a matter of being hard or soft. It is not a matter of being tough or easy. It is, rather, a matter of choosing effective means for encouraging a person to change directions for his life. The kind of punishment we have administered to ´prisoners is grossly ineffective and not calculated to produce constructive change in human beings.

Surely dangerous people must be confined and there must be penalties for crime. But the vindictive elements in our punishment and the indifference of both prison and community which has characterized our response to the criminal offender hurts everyone. Conversely, everyone is helped if our basic policy and program are designed not to tear a man down but to provide a situation wherein he can build himself up.

The concept of punishment deserves to be abandoned. If this should prove impossible, the concept must then be filled with new meaning. If it means retribution or retaliation, it is intrinsically immoral. We should leave punishment to God who alone knows how the mystery of evil can and will be finally overcome.

Newman R. Gaugler, "The Church and the Criminal: Can They Be Reconciled?" **Quaker Life**, April 1976, pp. 10-11.

But prisons are not going to effect reconciliation now or ever. They do not heal, correct, build, grow human beings according to Judeo-Christian values. As Jerome Miller, who changed the Massachusetts Division of Youth Services which was notorious for its mistreatment of the young, said: "It is impossible to reform a prison. It never happens and it never will...because it rests on violence to, and repression of deviants...it is impossible to sustain reform within systems that are based on violence."

I hear Miller explicating Jesus' text from Isaiah. Incarceration and punishment and indignity are not Judeo-Christian answers to the question of the wounded brother or sister, either offender or victim.

Finally, Christian theology brings the existence, the condition and the continuance of the prison system back to us. "Am I my brother's keeper?" must be answered by the principles and teaching of the Judeo-Christian heritage. The answer will be: "No, you are your brother's brother, your brother's sister."

Theology in its truth-telling, its witnessing, and prophesying must lay bare the evil, the inhumanity, the indignity done. But more, we must allow that truth to penetrate into our own souls. We are called to accountability and to involvement in reconciliation and healing....

Persons are only cured by love. No structure can accomplish what one compassionate person can do, and that is the task of us all, each at our own particular level and through the particular gift that we possess and are. For the interim, until we wipe out these useless, exorbitantly expensive "poorhouses of the 20th century" which we call prisons, intelligent alternatives to incarceration are the interim answer.

Within the past nine years five major commissions have examined the U.S. correctional problem. The most recent and important report is **Corrections**, by the National Advisory Commission on Criminal Justice Standards and Goals. This commission tried to formulate for the first time (please note!) *national* criminal justice standards and goals for crime reduction and prevention. Most unfortunately, its findings are not binding on national and local prison empires. But the recommendations will be adopted if the individual state or locality so chooses.

Citizen education and action will decide. Surely those of us whose Judeo-Christian theology calls for humane changes will be among those taking responsibility. As one recommendation calls for a 10-year moratorium on prison building, we can provide community-based alternatives to reintegrate the offender. No societal task is more necessary, more immediately pressing or closer to the goal of a healing community.

RECONCILIATION, NOT ALIENATION

The one ethical principle on which Christian ethicists are united is that the supreme purpose of all human conduct toward others should be benevolent love. Leading Jewish moralists and secular humanists concur. All agree also that every human being, regardless of character, age or ability must be treated with respect for his or her human dignity....

However, on this matter of criminal justice, Protestants and Catholics alike here usually have gone along with the individualistic American culture. With rare exceptions our processes of criminal justice seek to rehabilitate the offender alone, if at all, often in prison where he is isolated from the community in which he will live after release. Such a process strangely ignores the realities of human existence as known to biblical faith and to modern anthropology and psychology as well.

Commission of a crime in itself is evidence of a serious alienation or breach already existing in the community, a rupture which the crime has now further aggravated. The task of justice is now a task of reconciliation, of healing, of social restoration...

Remembering our Lord's ministry to a dying thief, even while he was himself enduring the last agonies of fiendish torture, and recalling his admonitions to us to visit the imprisoned, dare we do less and call ourselves Christians?

L. Harold DeWolf, ''Dare Our Ministry Be Less Than Christ's?''
National Catholic Reporter, April 6, 1976.

Rehabilitation can only begin and ultimately succeed in the simplest and the hardest way: the Word must become flesh in us, too, so that the ex-offender and the offender can see in us, in our community, love and concern made flesh, not in our words only, but in our real acceptance, our risk-taking, our opening the door, our giving the job, our being what we profess: those who love — as Jesus loves us — not with justice, but with the love that forgives, a concept never really tried in criminal justice. It could be the distinctive, revolutionary contribution of Christians to a solution.

VIEWPOINT 10

Isolate Criminals Until Age 35

William Buckley

William F. Buckley is a leading spokesman for conservative ideas and politics. He is the editor of the **National Review** and the author of various books that deal with social and political issues. Frequently he can be seen conducting interviews with key people about national events on the National Public Television program **Firing Line**.

Consider the following questions while reading:

1. The author compares the punishment philosophies of James Wilson and Ernest van den Haag. How do they differ?
2. Why does Mr. Buckley propose that criminals be isolated until age 35?

William F. Buckley, "Isolate Hard Criminals Until Age 35?" **Washington Star Syndicate**, 1976.

From Hong Kong, there is a report on the final hours on earth of two young men convicted of brutal murders. They were given the traditional last meal of their choice. Then they were driven to the prison compound, and a firing squad did its duty. A fairly routine experience, with this exception: The whole of it was televised and shown during prime time.

The authorities in Hong Kong have announced their determination to do something to check the growing crime rate. Well, they have certainly come up with something original.

It would, of course, be more palatable if someone might arrange it so that the program went out on closed-circuit TV into the living quarters only of potential murderers. But it is this kind of fine tuning that always eludes one. The kind that raises disagreement between men of such original thought as James Wilson of Harvard and Ernest van den Haag of the New School for Social Research.

Wilson's book, published last year, is called **Thinking About Crime**, Van den Haag's, published a few weeks ago, is called **Punishing Criminals: Concerning a Very Old and Painful Question**. It is a revelation, precisely because Van den Haag is prepared first to digest current findings about penology; then, because he is sufficiently the craftsman, to give these findings plainly, and, finally, because he is superbly skilled at asking just the right questions, anticipating the most dogged superstitions.

He and Wilson agree on most of the fundamental points, notably that we have made no advances whatever in the art of rehabilitation; that, although the incidence of crime may be greater among the poor, this generality sheds no light whatever on the causal relation between poverty and crime.

Both believe that sentences should be determinate, with, however, an intriguing difference. Van den Haag believes a prison sentence should be based on what he calls a ''categorical basis.'' Here is what he is talking about:

Forty-five percent of all murders are done by people

less than 25 years old and three-quarters of all crime by people who are under 30. Now, since we do not know anything about rehabilitation, and since we have irrefutable evidence that recidivism is responsible for a huge percentage of crime, we are faced with the problem: How should we deal with a repeat offender found guilty of a second violent crime?

WHO SHOULD LIVE BEHIND BARS?

The 1960s were years in which corrections experts were trying hard to persuade the public that prisons are unsuited to the task of rehabilitating criminals. The persuading was easy, for this is one notion on which there is much agreement in criminal justice circles. Few observers any longer believe that prisons do very much to mend the majority of persons confined in them. On the contrary, it is generally accepted that a novice criminal sent to prison will learn there how better to commit crime rather than how to avoid committing crimes.

Consequently, when the public was told that rehabilitation is a myth, there was no one to disagree.

If prisons do not rehabilitate, then criminals should not be kept in prisons. This was the second stage of the correctional propaganda. On this, there has been growing disagreement of late. Community corrections programs were proposed as alternatives to incarceration....

Soon, in such widely separated places as California, Massachusetts and the District of Columbia, police and prosecutors were complaining that a lot of dangerous criminals were out on the streets committing new crimes while "serving" their sentences in community corrections modes.

A necessary risk, correctional experts reported, for without rehabilitation, imprisonment is nothing but warehousing of men.

Now, when first heard, the "warehousing of men" is as repulsive a notion as "community corrections" is inviting. But rehabilitation is not the only purpose of prisons. Retribution, deterrence, and immobilization, as well as rehabilitation, are coequal, traditional functions of prisons, and "warehousing," is just a substitute term for immobilization. Temporarily restricting the ability of a criminal to commit a crime by keeping him incarcerated is a legitimate and appropriate function of prisons.

This doesn't mean that everyone who commits a crime has to go to jail. If it did, most of our population soon would be there. What we do need is to concentrate on those few categories of criminals who have infringed so much on the freedom of our lifestyles in recent times.

We need to prevent that class of crimes which cause people to bar the windows of their homes, which make citizens afraid to walk their streets at night, which force us to carry correct change if we want to ride buses or buy gasoline at night....

This doesn't mean that we need to send a lot of criminals to prison for life. Prison does not rehabilitate, but maturing does. Eighty-one percent of persons arrested for rape, robbery and burglary are under 25 years of age; 90 percent are under 30.

Before you object to imprisoning them for awhile, ask yourself: Who would you rather have living behind some kind of bars?

Jerry V. Wilson, former Washington, D.C. police chief, **Minneapolis Star**, September 23, 1975.

Let us suppose that at age 18 he robbed at gunpoint and was given five years, paroled after three. Six months later he robs again at gunpoint, and we are fortunate enough to catch him. He is convicted. Normally, he would be given the five years and, in some states, the two years unserved from the previous sentence for violating his parole would be reinstated. Here, he would be eligible for fresh parole at about age 25.

Under the categorical rule of Van den Haag, the procedure would be changed. Until age 25, he would be kept in an orthodox prison in which he would be simultaneously punished and sequestered. Of course, after that he could go somewhere else. Throw in your own specifications here, if you will — to an island somewhere, perhaps; to a reservation to which he would be free to take his family and given a kind of insular liberty.

> **If we mean business about reducing crime, let us accept the elementary usefulness of a prison as a place of imprisonment. The reformers are fond of saying that it "does no good" to put a man behind bars for 10 to 15 years. They are wrong. For that period of 10 to 15 years, at least, the criminal is out of circulation. He is not robbing, assaulting raping, killing or stealing.**

James J. Kilpatrick, "The Way To Reduce Crime," **Nation's Business**, April 1975, p. 8.

The point is that he would not be permitted to re-enter normal society until age 35 — because it is after that age that the impulse to criminality drops sharply. Van den Haag calculates, roughly, that if his plan were invoked, injustice would fall on 40 percent of those sequestered. That is, 60 percent of those sequestered would indeed commit violent crimes again. But, like the Hong Kong television viewers, we cannot know which 60 percent they are.

Wilson declines to go along with a plan that would accept guaranteed injustice. Van den Haag, in his fascinating book, tells us that we must revise the idea of justice; we must focus our concern on those statistically predictable victims who would now be spared, at the cost of the physical detention of two-time offenders, 40 percent of whom would not have broken the law again. Which 40 percent?

Once in a very long while a book takes the reader through intricate philosophical and sociological thickets with assurance and cogency. Van den Haag has done it, and his book, and Wilson's, should be closely read by everyone in America who is the likely victim of a crime, which means about 70 percent of the population.

I Favor Abolishing Prisons

John O. Boone

John O. Boone is the Urban Affairs Director of WNAC-TV in Boston. He was formerly Commissioner of Correction for the Commonwealth of Massachusetts, Superintendent of the Lorton Correction Complex, Lorton, Va., Corrections Officer at the U.S. Penitentiary, Atlanta, and instructor in Criminal Justice at Boston University Law School.

As you read consider the following questions:

1. Why does the author favor abolishing prisons?
2. Does the author think prisons are part of a racial problem?

John Boone, ''Prisons Should Be Abolished,'' **Fortune News**, May, 1975, p. 2.

Q. You have often used the phrase, "persons who should have limited movement." Could you please explain this statement?

A. I have used this phrase defensively in response to questions about "dangerousness" and the character of persons who should be confined. Imprisonment is the ultimate instrument for the limiting of one's movement. Probation and parole are other instruments. But for the most part these instruments have been used inappropriately. Prisons have been used to limit the movement of persons labeled as "dangerous," "psychotic" or "disturbed," a labeling process which began in the community, in the bad schools and continued through each stage of the criminal justice system. The result has been the destruction of thousands of lives. We have been so concerned with containment, with limiting movement, that we haven't looked for the real troubles in people, in communities, in our social and economic system....

Q. What are the reasons why you advocate a reduction in the number of prisons in our country?

A. I must refer you to the Campaign's proposal for a more detailed statement. In short however, we advocate a reduction in the number of prisons because it is clear that the only consistent accomplishment of the prison system has been failure. Prisons are crime manufacturing concerns; do nothing to deter "criminal" behavior; are dehumanizing and brutalizing to the people forced to live in them; and serve only the vested interests in this country, the politically powerful, the rich and ruling class, the peddlers of steel, concrete, tear gas and other prison hardware. And we maintain these institutions at the same time that viable, more humane, at least potentially more effective and certainly less expensive alternatives already exist.

Q. How do you answer critics who cite the rise in crime as a reason for increasing the number of prisons?

A. An ignorant public, and public officials, punish themselves by looking at the crime rate in terms of the need for more prisons. The crime rate has been increasing despite an already heavy use of prisons. Prisons don't reduce crime; if anything they produce

72

better criminals. Instead of such a knee-jerk reaction to increased crime (the fear of which is consciously promoted by the FBI, the police, some of the media and some politicians) we need to look into the community for the forces that make crime. We need to develop a means of coping with the problems in that community, but with our national and local priorities being what they are, it is unlikely that anything serious will happen to affect the problems which plague our communities.

NICE NAMES FOR UNPLEASANT REALITIES

Incarceration is punishment, and it almost invariably brings with it brutality; the brutality may come from fellow convicts or from the guards or authorities, but it comes. Incarceration is not as horrible as maiming or torture or execution, but it is painful. Calling it by another name is nonsense, as is calling prisons "correctional institutions" and "reform schools," as is calling guards "correctional officers," prisoners "inmates" or "residents," and solitary confinement "behavior adjustment." Nice names for unpleasant realities avail naught. They certainly do not make the convicts feel better.

Charles Owen Rice, "Prisons Making Matters Worse," **Catholic Bulletin**, April 7, 1975.

Q. How do you go about selling the idea of prison abolition?

A. We need to create an atmosphere in which abolition can take place. It will require a firm alliance between those groups, individuals and organizations which understand that this will not happen overnight. Just as the slavery abolitionist movement extended over decades, we must be prepared to struggle at length. But we must start, we must fuel the fires, we must make the alliance that will gain us victory.

73

PRISONS ARE MUSEUMS OF THE PAST

Penitentiaries dated from the end of the 18th century, when Quaker reformers in Pennsylvania had given a new twist to the standard notion that people became criminals because they were corrupt. Whereas the Puritans had argued that corruption was inherent in the criminal, an extreme result of mankind's innate depravity, the Quakers maintained that corruption was communicated to the criminal by weaknesses in the social order, stemming from the alleged moral breakdown of the family, the churches and the schools.

If this were the case, one had to be removed from these corrupting social influences, and one would shed one's acquired criminal tendencies....

The very name of the institution in which this shedding of criminality was to occur was important: it was quite literally a house of penance. In silence and solitary confinement, with only the Bible to read, the inmate would reflect on his past life and repent....

Contemporary prisons are no longer buttressed by the social context and the psychological presuppositions which called them forth....

Prisons are museums of that age, commemorating the dreams, sometimes naive, of a more homogeneous and simple society. Museums are to be visited and looked at, but it is highly doubtful that any useful purpose is served by condemning large numbers of people to live out the hopes of the early 19th century.

Robert M. Senkewicz, ''Early American Innocence and the 'Modern' Prison,'' **America**, April 24, 1976, p. 353.

Q. Is prison — as we know it — a class or a racial struggle?

A. In the sense that Black and Spanish-speaking and Native American people on all levels get a bad deal in the criminal justice process, from judges and lawyers and other influential people who are almost always white, there can be no doubt that racism has a massive effect. But, when you look at prisons, who do you find there. Not only Black people, Spanish-speaking people, Native Americans, but also white people, poor white people, white people who have been subject to the same economic oppression as the Black, Brown and Red prisoners with whom they are locked away. I believe that it is vital for all of us, and especially for people in prison to understand this, and to find the ways of cutting across ethnic lines to unite for the fight against class oppression. The fight against prisons, and for a better life, must be a class struggle. We must unite if we are to succeed.

Distinguishing Fact From Opinion

This discussion exercise is designed to promote experimentation with one's ability to distinguish between fact and opinion. It is a fact, for example, that the United States was militarily involved in the Vietnam War. But to say this involvement served the interests of world peace is an opinion or conclusion. Future historians will agree that American soldiers fought in Vietnam, but their interpretations about the causes and consequences of the war will probably vary greatly.

Some of the following statements are taken from readings in this chapter and some have other origins. Consider each statement carefully. Mark **O** for any statement you feel is an opinion or interpretation of the facts. Mark **F** for any statement you believe is fact. Then discuss and compare your judgments with those of other class members.

O = OPINION
F = FACT

_____ 1. White collar criminals receive sufficient punishment when their crimes are made public.

_____ 2. The United States has a higher gun murder rate than do countries with strict gun control laws.

_____ 3. An important cause of crime in America is the decline of individual responsibility.

_____ 4. Criminals are the product of environment, not heredity.

_____ 5. Swift and sure punishment of criminals would reduce crime.

_____ 6. Prisons cause more crime than they prevent.

_____ 7. Most criminals can be rehabilitated.

_____ 8. Use of the death penalty would reduce crime by eliminating hard core criminals and murderers.

_____ 9. Most criminals are the products of bad parents.

_____ 10. Public safety is more important than the individual rights of criminals.

_____ 11. Most prison inmates, when set free, commit additional crimes.

_____ 12. Violent crime is more destructive to American society than white collar crime.

_____ 13. Poverty is the most important cause of crime.

_____ 14. Most first time murderers never commit a second murder.

CHAPTER

DEALING WITH JUVENILE OFFENDERS

Children Should Be Held Responsible for Their Crimes

Ernest van den Haag

Ernst van den Haag is both a psychoanalyst and a noted social critic. He is a Lecturer in Psychology and Sociology at the New School for Social Research and Adjunct Professor of Social Philosophy at New York University. He is the author of numerous books and articles on a wide range of social problems.

Use the following questions to assist your reading:

1. Why does the author think 14 year old offenders should be held as responsible for their crimes as adults?
2. What inequities does he cite in the sentencing of juvenile offenders?
3. What problem does the author believe results when juvenile offenders are treated leniently?

Ernest van den Haag, **Punishing Criminals: Concerning a Very Old and Painful Question** (New York: Basic Books, Inc., 1975), pp. 173-75, 249. From **Punishing Criminals: Concerning a Very Old and Painful Question**, by Ernest van den Haag, (c) Basic Books, Inc., Publishers, New York.

Children surely should not be held responsible for their conduct to the extent adults are. But should we regard sixteen-year-olds or even fourteen-year-olds as children? They do engage in all the activities — except, possibly, work — adults engage in, including crime. Indeed, we make it increasingly hard for juveniles to work and increasingly easy for them to do almost anything else. There is little reason left for not holding juveniles responsible under the same laws that apply to adults. The victim of a fifteen-year-old mugger is as much mugged as the victim of a twenty-year-old mugger, the victim of a fourteen-year-old murderer or rapist is as dead or as raped as the victim of an older one. The need for social defense or protection is the same. Juveniles may be held in custody separately from adults and perhaps subjected to a special custodial authority. But the process of adjudication and the law should be the same. A letter in the **New York Times Sunday Magazine** (Feb. 16, 1975) lends support to this view from an unexpected quarter.

> The (juvenile) court purports to address the psychological and social deprivations of all children — that is, to "treat" and "rehabilitate" children whose lives are less than optimal. This "treatment" rationale means that the children who have never committed any crime, but who have "problems" (running away from uncaring homes, refusing to attend worse schools) are confined together in the same detention facilities with adolescents who torture, sodomize, rape and murder. The young murderer usually stays no more than nine months in training school. The so-called PINS children (Person in Need of Supervision —- runaways, truants, etc.) will stay 18 months or longer because their parents, who brought them to court in the first place, do not want them.
>
> The length of time that a young criminal is confined ought to be determined primarily by the nature of the offense he has committed, with due consideration for the reduced capacity of children to formulate criminal intent, past records, and the fact that the mere passage of time is more likely to alter the behavior of a 15-year-old than of a 30-year-old. Neither the juvenile court nor any agency should have the power to confine any child (with the possible exception of a suicidal child) who has not violated the criminal law, no matter what his problems.
>
> Elimination of PINS children from court jurisdiction altogether and a sentencing system for child criminals which primarily reflect the seriousness of the crimes, are reforms that are long, long overdue. They are vociferously resisted, however, by those misguided humanitarians who insist that the coercive power of a court should be a conduit for social services and that "treatment" is holy.
>
> Rena K. Uviller, Director Juvenile Rights Project
> American Civil Liberties Union New York City

A further illustration (**New York Times**, December 6, 1974, p. 43):

"This is his fourth arrest," Detective Walker said, referring to the 14-year-old boy whose name was withheld in keeping with Family Court laws intended to protect the youth. "All four cases were for assault and robbery only in two cases the result was death."

"He didn't seem shook up," the detective said. "He knows he can only get 18 months. We can't cope with this court system. They're not giving them enough time. There's no punishment."

"THEY CAN'T DO ANYTHING TO ME"

James Franz Arbeiter was twice found guilty by Missiouri juries of stabbing Mrs. Nancy Zanzone to death when she surprised him in the burglary of her apartment. He showed no remorse, boasting "I'm only 15 years old. They can't do anything to me." Unfortunately, he was right. After conviction by two juries, the Missouri Supreme Court freed him on legal technicalities. Less than a year later, he pleaded guilty to burglary and weapon charges. After serving less than three years of a six year sentence, he was charged with the fatal shooting of a night club owner and of forcing his female companion to perform an illicit sex act.

Phyllis Schlafly, "Crime and Punishment," **The Phyllis Schlafly Report**, March 1976.

Anyone under fifteen years old, regardless of how heinous the crime, receives a maximum of eighteen months detention. All too often young boys are simply released back into the community and the school system....

After the age of thirteen, juveniles should be treated as adults for indictment, trial and sentencing purposes. Once they are in penal institutions or in confinement, they may be held separately and treated differently. But not to hold them responsible for their offenses or not to punish them is to license and encourage juveniles to commit offenses. To be sure, most juvenile offenders come from particularly trying backgrounds and home situations. However, there is no evidence that such home situations become worse compared with what they were twenty years ago. Yet there are more offenders among juveniles. They are the product of the leniency of the law — of the privilege granted them — as much as of anything else.

"**What possible alibi can you have, Sir, for leaving your car where my disadvantaged young client could steal it?**"

Abolish Juvenile Prisons

Jerome Miller

Dr. Jerome Miller is presently the Commissioner of Children and Youth for the Commonwealth of Pennsylvania. He made history in his field when he was Commissioner of Youth Services for the Commonwealth of Massachusetts. His innovative efforts in that state serve as the basis for this interview with the **Fortune News**.

Use the following questions to assist your reading:

1. How does the author think violent juvenile offenders should be treated?
2. Why is he critical of present correctional facilities for juveniles?
3. What does the author mean when he uses the terms ''status offender''?

Jerome Miller, ''On Caged Children,'' **Fortune News**, October, 1975, p. 4.

Q. You removed children from cages in an innovative program when you were in Massachusetts. How did you proceed, politically and pragmatically, to achieve this?

A. It would be a difficult and perhaps confusing process to try to outline all the political and pragmatic strategies to getting out of institutions for juvenile offenders. I guess rather simply, that we decided that we could no longer look the other way as children were being destroyed by our institutional systems and that we had to act rather affirmatively and quickly if we were to confront the contradiction of sustaining a system of "care" which despite all the rhetoric and overlay of "rehabilitation", was in fact destroying young lives. Once that moral decision was made, the pragmatic and political issues, though of real concern, were of secondary importance....

Q. When a youth is violent and presents a danger to the safety of the community, what is your recommendation in the handling of the juvenile?

A. I have no quarrel with those that say that there are some youth who are indeed "violent" and who cannot be loose in the community. I think, however, that the category is much overstated and over-exaggerated and that in fact many of the violent offenders are products of our juvenile correctional system. For the truly violent youthful offender, however, I don't see any reason why we cannot begin to create and offer the kinds of options we have already provided for the past 50 or 75 years for the violent offender of the upper middle-class. Violent youth in juvenile corrections are for the most part children of the poor and although we spend a great deal of time, effort and money in further destroying them in our correctional system, there is little evidence that we have been successful in curbing their violence or in any way insuring further public safety. If a juvenile has to be in a secure setting, or in a program that can guarantee security — with one or two staff on his arm at all times on the street, I don't see any reason why the program cannot be small, caring and individualized and offer the kinds of programs and demand the kind of accountability from the programs that we have always sought for the dangerous offender of the upper middle-class. We've always been able to handle those "dangerous" youth with decency and humanity and still guarantee public safety. For those who need a secure setting or a secure program, there is no reason for it to be a monolithic, bureaucratic, single sex, violent bureaucracy which we call the prison or the training school. I feel strongly that we can design small 10 or 12 bed units that can guarantee security and individualized care and that indeed beyond that we can devise programs in the community that guarantee security through adequate staffing. For what it costs to keep a juvenile in a locked secure setting, we can hire one or two staff to be with the juvenile in a variety of settings around the clock, thereby providing public safety without relegating a person to a human warehouse. I must stress however, that my experience with so called violent offenders is that there aren't many around, that most of those in the present juvenile correctional system defined as violent are in fact products of that system or management problems within that system. We have created a system which produces the very thing it's supposed to "treat".

Q. Has there been a substantial difference in the distribution of juvenile justice for boys and girls?

A. There certainly has. Most girls detained in training school and detention centers throughout the nation are detained for crimes that would not be crimes if they were adults — that is for status offenses, such as truancy, runaway, ungovernability, stubbornness, etc. I strongly support the position on the National Council on Crime and Delinquency to remove status offenses from the jurisdiction of the juvenile justice system altogether.

Q. From your perception, how have you seen institutional life affect children?

A. Believe it or not, I have seen some good institutions (though not very many) and I have seen a lot of destructive institutions. I think the issue is not so much the institution, as it is the fact that large institutions with coerced populations generally tend to make decisions at the expense of the clientele and to the best interests of the staff. As a result, cumulatively, over time they become repressive and destructive. Now and then a charismatic superintendent or director of treatment can pick a program up by its bootstraps and make it work

85

CAUSES OF
JUVENILE CRIME

Those who fill America's jails and prisons are notoriously impotent in politics; juvenile lawbreakers have two strikes against them. And America's system of juvenile justice shows it.

The juvenile justice system was begun at the turn of the century to single out youths for special attention. But more often than not, the system has failed the young. Resources and facilities have lagged far behind needs. And despite the advice of those who work in the field, the public concentrates efforts on courts and detention facilities rather than on juvenile crime prevention programs....

Ironically, juvenile experts say they know the causes of juvenile delinquency and who is most likely to commit crime. Recent studies show high correlations between juvenile offenders and those who fail in school....

A national study shows that eight million youths are going to drop out of school in the next decade. Eighty-five per cent of those who will develop serious behavioral problems will be from this group.

Society provides no alternative to success in school for juveniles.... If they fail in school, they fail in life. And it is those who feel they are failures that turn to crime to prove they are not.

Thomas C. Fox, "Juvenile 'Justice' Fails the Young and Fails Society," **National Catholic Reporter**, April 16, 1976.

for a while. However, it's been my experience that large institutions have a difficult and impossible task in *sustaining* decent programs for children. I guess that to the degree institutions are freely chosen by the clientele who wish to be there and can leave at will to that degree, institutions might work. However, that is not the case with most delinquent youngsters and probably will not be the case in the foreseeable future. As a result it seems to me that we have to provide more individualized programs with the likelihood that we can fit the program to the needs of the kids rather than vice versa.

Q. Also, what is the substantive difference for children now in Mass. as compared to before the structural change?

A. I think the most important difference in Massachusetts is that whereas in 1969 we maybe had a half-dozen programs to chose from, in 1975 Massachusetts can choose from 250 or more different programs for delinquent children with the chance of optimizing the kids' possibilities for decent care.

Q. What do you perceive to be the major factors (causes) of delinquency in children?

A. There are so many cultural, social and individual that I think it would be foolhardy to focus inordinately on any one or two. I guess there are some responsibilities which society has regarding providing a certain level of human decency and stability to the social systems within which children are raised and have to function. Such factors go well beyond the scope of juvenile corrections and relate to issues such as poverty, illness, racism, etc. By the same token, however, I do not believe that we in juvenile corrections can get so easily off the hook by saying that it is beyond our capacity to do anything about the problem. It seems to me that at the very least we can insure that we do not make the problem worse — which is precisely what the present system does. I'd be reasonably satisfied if I could be sure that the juvenile correctional system in the United States does not destroy human beings and make them less likely to function after our "treatment". In that sense I am somewhat of a pessimist about "rehabilitation". I feel I do have some hope that decent care can result in kids leading fuller lives.

Q. If this program can be implemented in Mass., could it succeed in other states?

87

A. Yes. I am frequently told that it couldn't succeed in states like New York which are much larger. I think it could. If it couldn't, there's no reason why it shouldn't succeed in at least 39 of the 50 states since Massachusetts is the tenth largest.

Q. What do you think we can reasonably expect from the incarceration of children for periods of 18 months to three or more years?

A. I think we can expect to produce career criminals.

Q. In most states, children are locked up for non-criminal offenses — referred to as status offenders: truants, runaways, unwanted, etc. What happens to these kids?

A. They are introduced to the criminal career process and more likely than not will be less able to make it following their detention than previous to their detention. One of the sound findings from the Harvard Center for Criminal Justice study of the Massachusetts system is that to the degree youngsters are detained early in the process, to that degree they are likely to repeat and go on to further crimes. One might think this is related to the myth that youngsters are detained on the seriousness of their crime. However, the Harvard Study shows further that the decision around detention is not made on the basis of the crime for the most part, but is made on the basis of social class and the availability of detention slots in locked settings. The rush to coerce and lock up early in the process more likely than not guarantees a recycling of the youngster in the system.

A Case of Juvenile Leniency

Edward N. Costikyan

Edward N. Costikyan is a member of the Association of the Bar of the City of New York, the American Bar Association, and a Fellow of the American College of Trial Lawyers.

Think of the following questions while you read:

1. What problem is the author attempting to draw attention to in this reading?
2. What does the author feel is most needed to stop the coddling of juvenile offenders?

Edward N. Costikyan, "Assault With Intent To Main," **New York**, May 31, 1976, pp. 7-8. Copyright (c) 1976 by the NYM Corp. Reprinted with the permission of **New York** Magazine.

On January 2, 1976, a sixteen-year-old boy was on his way home at 11:50 P.M. (As his father, when the events of that night were related to me I initially wondered why he was out that late, until I remembered my own nighttime schedule at the same age.) At 84th Street and Second Avenue he was attacked by a young hoodlum (white, if you are interested), age fifteen, who, with three confederates, had just assaulted three other citizens within four minutes. There was no attempt to rob, just sheer brute aggression intent upon maiming, the end result of which was a blackened but, thank God, undamaged eye, a bruised face and ribs, two cracked fingers, and a victim hard put to understand why this should have happened.

A passerby came to the rescue when he heard my son's shouts for help. The police, responding to alarms from the first assault, arrived in time to terminate the fourth. The ''perpetrator'' was apprehended.

The ''perpetrator'' had had three prior arrests in five months. Charges arising from the first two arrests were apparently dropped. The third was for an assault of the same nature — the objective also was an eye of the victim — and took place on November 24, 1975. The ''perpetrator'' was paroled pending trial on that assault, and so was back on the street committing the assault on my son even before his trial for the previous one.

After the assault on my son, the ''perpetrator,'' again on parole pending trial, was convicted of the November 24 assault. His sentence on that charge was suspended and he was released, notwithstanding his arrest for another assault even before his trial for the first. The ''perpetrator'' was, according to the representation made to the court, a teen-age alcoholic who attempted mayhem only when he got drunk. This was the same story the first judge had accepted in paroling him.

There is reason to believe that anyone had brought to the first judge's attention the fact that since the arrest of the young man he had assaulted four citizens in five minutes, had been apprehended, had cursed out the police, and had threatened the passerby and my son with vengeance. The Family Court just doesn't work that way, and since its proceedings are private, there was no way for the defendant's later victims to tell the court these facts.

Of the four victims of the second set of assaults, only my son pressed charges. One, a bus driver, didn't "want to get involved." One simply walked away. One was a visitor from Egypt to whom American attitudes about young juvenile delinquents made no sense.

There were court appearances — four for my son, three for the passerby, and two for the police. During one of them, I casually asked a social worker whether the defendant had a prior record. I learned of the three prior arrests — this was the fourth. I learned from the police that the defendant was one of a group of young delinquents who had terrorized the block for months.

The defendant pleaded guilty, with my son's consent, to a charge of attempted assault, but also explicitly admitted the factual charges which constituted actual, premeditated assault.

I had expected the prosecution to be prepared to report to the judge the defendant's prior record, the four assaults in five minutes, the terrorization of the block, and the threats to my son and the passerby-witness. But no one had told the judge about any of it, until I did shortly before the hearing. I told him of the prior arrest and the prior adjudication. There was no information about it in his file, and the prosecutor went to another office on another floor to attempt to verify what I told him. He returned shortly and confirmed that my information about the prior arrest and adjudication was correct. At the hearing, the social workers did not volunteer any information about the earlier adjudicated assault until the prosecutor raised the issue. Then it was weakly confirmed.

Nor, so far as I am aware, was the court advised that this was one of four assaults in five minues or that there had been three earlier arrests within five months, or that the "perpetrator" shouted threats of revenge, in the police station, against my son and the courageous passerby who stuck his neck out to save somebody else's sight.

PAMPERING YOUTHFUL CRIMINALS

The reluctance of our courts to treat children as criminals is encouraging stealing, assault, rape and even murder on the idea that juveniles should be coddled but not punished....

Kids who are tough enough to wreck churches and schools, hold up service stations, snatch women's purses, beat up old men and women and commit robbery and murder are old enough to have a public trial. Under the present system they are shielded from trials or any court action which would treat them as criminals....

If the public is to be protected from lawbreakers, the present system, which pampers youthful criminals, is long overdue for a change. The public safety should have priority over the inefficient theories of the do-gooders.

Paul Clement, letter to the editor in **Minneapolis Star**, March 23, 1974.

Of course, I cannot be sure, because after the guilty plea my son, his mother, and I were excluded from the courtroom when the sentencing was to take place. So far as I could tell, however, the court's procedures did not seem to be intended to bring these facts to the judge's attention. Not even the prior "adjudication" was initially reported to the judge. Instead, there was another recommendation for "probation."

If the court was made aware of the young man's record, its action was even more inexplicable.

For, after holding the defendant until the end of the day, the judge paroled the defendant again because — again — he was an alcoholic and committed assaults only when he was drunk.

The young "alcoholic" who attempts to commit

92

mayhem only when he drinks is therefore back on the streets, being "treated" for adolescent alcoholism. I wonder when the next assault will take place.

All of this loving-kingness for the young may have made sense once. But times have changed. Children mature earlier, yet even teen-age murderers can apparently receive no more than a maximum of a year and a half in a reformatory. It is clear that the practices of an earlier era are pursued as if the courts were still dealing only with youthful shenanigans.

"I CAN KILL BECAUSE I'M ONLY 14"

A 14-year-old knows the worst that can happen is 18 months in a training school,... He thinks, I can kill a man because I'm 14. So you have murderers and rapists returned to the street in no time. If he's older, his parents come in and lie about his age, and say they can't find his birth certificate. They should knock down the whole age barrier, depending on the type of crime and the past history of the kid involved. It should be like intox driving; the first time it's a misdemeanor, the second time it's a felony. The way it is now, it's a big game.

Brooklyn police detective Hans Fredericks quoted in "They Think, 'I Can Kill Because I'm 14'," **New York Times Magazine**, January 19, 1975, p. 11.

The end result has had a devastating effect on the life of the city. Indeed, the Family Court and its philosophy that everyone is curable has played a significant role in the deterioration of our social fabric. If the city is to survive, that court needs new attitudes, certainly new procedures, a new sense of its social purpose, and some perception of the impact of its practices upon the rest of the city.

Probably what it needs most of all is press coverage.

The end result of excluding the press from the courtroom is not a matter of conjecture. The evidence is all over New York City in the form of dangerous young people preying on the citizenry and driving many of them out of town.

This does not mean needlessly broadcasting the names of mischievous children. But it should mean that the judges who sit on that court should no longer be forced or permitted to function in anonymity. The Family Court and its predecessors have been protected from public scrutiny for generations — presumably to protect the young. Alas, the protection of the young has produced a distortion of justice, and it is time to take a long and hard look at the end results of judicial privacy.

Juvenile Offenders Need Understanding, Not Punishment

David Rothenberg

David Rothenberg is the executive director of the Fortune Society, an organization which he founded in 1967. He is a member of the Board of Directors of the National Council on Crime and Delinquency and he was a member of the Attica Observer's Committee.

As you read try to answer the following questions:

1. What does the author think of ''permissiveness'' as the major cause of juvenile crime?
2. How does the author relate children's institutions and prisons to battered and abused children?
3. Why does the author think the punishment concept produces just the opposite of the desired result?

David Rothenberg, ''Punishment + Punishment = Crime,'' **Fortune News**, December, 1974, p. 2.

Parental permissiveness is the largest contributing cause of crime, states a public survey in a recent **New York Times** poll. Other major factors, as perceived by the man and woman on the street, are drugs, unemployment, court laxity, lack of law enforcement, and poverty — in that order.

It is the frequent use of the word "permissiveness" which hovers over much of the public's interpretations of causes of crime as seen in the **Times'** survey and elsewhere. Subsequently, this idea has often been utilized and nurtured by politicians as they make the sounds of cure and prevention.

My past 7 years at the Fortune Society, meeting with thousands of ex-convicts from around the country, would lead me to the exact opposite conclusion of the **Times'** survey. I have found the "permissiveness" theory a fallacious one and the subsequent suggested solutions tend to be political pacifiers rather than problem-solvers.

Most adult convicts and ex-convicts have decidedly not come from permissive home situations. To the contrary, ex-cons as a group, tend to have had extremely abusive and/or neglectful childhoods.

If you seek a common denominator in our adult penitentiaries you could begin with child abuse, physical as well as emotional, racial, social, psychological and economic.

Some of the stories which I have heard from various ex-cons and prisoners stagger the sensibilities of an allegedly civilized population. Such childhood reminiscences include:

• Being placed in ice water with the windows open in mid-winter at 5 years of age.

• Told to lie still and not move for 30 minutes with the promise of a whipping if he did...an 8 year old.

• Being held by his feet, at 3 years of age, from an apartment window.

• Having been branded with hot irons and having his fingers placed in a toaster.

96

- A crawling baby placed in a crib, with a lid on it, so as to make it a tomb, and left for 8 months.

- Recollections of being tied to a chair by a drunken father and being whipped until the father was exhausted...age 5.

- Being locked in a closet at an orphanage where other children urinated and defecated on him.

Also traumatic, is the honest realization by some adult men that they never recall being hugged or carressed as children. Many were so visibly unwanted by their families (often one-parent families) that they were disposed of to state institutions which manufacture indifference in wholesale quantities.

"Revenge" rather than "permissiveness" is a word we should examine if we want to understand some of the causes of apparently senseless street crimes. Little children who absorb the hurt sometimes explode in a rage against a world which never noticed them. Often it takes years for the dynamite to go off.

Tales of recalled torture from so many ex-cons almost bend into one. The stories are so painful that I see people turning them off, not wanting to really hear or believe them. These stories almost become a cliche because they are so similar and recurring. But these lives are not cliches; they are a sub-culture of the battered and neglected child which we have ignored.

Our children's institutions and our adult prisons have been exaggerated extensions of such abuse and indifference. Our battered children become adult felons, and we show our first societal concern about them when they emerge in our headline with such names as Richard Speck and Charles Manson.

Our prisons are filled with men who were badly battered and frequently tortured children (either at home or in orphanages, training schools, child shelters, or reformatories). For insights on what happens to our battered female children we need only to examine our mental institutions. Our society, apparently, conditions women to internalize their hurt and hostility. In a self-destructive manner they end up in our self-perpetu-

97

TRAINING SCHOOLS

Training schools are part of the poverty apparatus. Most children in training schools are poor, as most children dealt with in the juvenile court system are poor.

A large number of children in training schools are young, about one-third being between 10 and 14 years old. Do they have to be in a correctional institution? I remember a visit to our office by the Secretary for Justice of New Zealand, "Good Lord, do you incarcerate 12 year-olds?" Not long ago the head counselor at the Bronx detention home wondered aloud to a New York Times reporter, "How do little kids from 7 to 10 years old get in here? Can you see a little kid like that being a danger to the community?"

It is not surprising that a disproportionate number of children in training schools are non-white. One study showed that the black children averaged almost 2 years younger than the whites at the time of admission than white children. Another study of New Jersey children before the juvenile courts found that about 70% of the children committed were first offenders.

In this country we speak so well of liberty, but more than any other country in the western world we deprive people of liberty, putting them into institutions. But we call it "correction" or "treatment." We are very egalitarian, and hate poverty. We conduct a war on poverty. But we have succeeded in institutionalizing poverty for millions of people; and we call it the welfare state. We in this country hate war, yet we are at war most of the time. But we don't call it that. We in this country beat our children, deprive them of growth, police them, put them in institutions. But that's not what we call it. What we say is that we protect them, we treat them, we love them. It's curious.

Sol Rubin, **Children As Victims of Institutionalization**, undated pamphlet by the National Council on Crime and Delinquency.

ating mental wards. Little boys are nurtured to externalize their feelings and the angry and punished male youths seek revenge against the world and comprise a great portion of our prison population.

As the public, the politician and the press cling to the erroneous notion that permissiveness is a dominant cause of crime, it would seem that it then justifies punishment as the appropriate bromide. Paradoxically, the punishment concept stimulates and perpetuates the anti-social attitudes and low self-esteem of many convicted felons. Neglect and abuse of the child is rationalized as "permissiveness" but that misnomer ignores the hurt of many offenders.

It is a sad commentary — as we examine our concept of criminal justice — that our need to punish is greater than our need to solve our problems. It has become almost socially chic conversation to exchange mugging and burglary tales. A sense of helplessness, about crime, seems to permeate the urban air. People are afraid to walk the streets, and the fears are often quite real. However, rather than coming to terms with many of the misguided values and communal hang-ups, we want instant solutions.

Along comes the politician with the promise — relevant or irrelevant — and we sign a blank check. "Get tough" is the solution, rather than "Get wise." If we punish enough, it may not reduce our chances of becoming a victim but at least we can get even with the perpetrator.

As long as we're asking the wrong questions, we shouldn't be surprised that we are getting the wrong answers.

99

16

Is Juvenile "Justice" Wishful Thinking?

Ron Horswell

The Plain Truth is a magazine published by Ambassador College in Pasadena, California. It claims to be a magazine of understanding and is written from the religious perspective of Garner Ted Armstrong and The World Wide Church of God.

Think of these questions while reading:

1. How does Ron Horswell describe the juvenile justice system?
2. What is a status offense?
3. The author describes the "Control Theory." What is it?

Ron Horswell, "Is Juvenile Justice Wishful Thinking?" **The Plain Truth**, January, 1977, p. 26-30.

THE SYSTEM

Just what is the juvenile justice system? The "system" is really a loose assortment of institutions designed to help, handle, or house kids in trouble, foster homes, special schools, "camps," and semi-prisons. All are fed their raw material of cantankerous, troubled, frightened, disoriented, and/or dangerous juveniles by the juvenile court.

In most large metropolitan areas, the infamous juvenile hall is also part of the "system." Juvenile hall is a place of waiting either for kids who are en route to the courtroom, or for kids who have had their day in court and are waiting for space to open up in the institution to which they have been assigned.

THE STATUS OFFENSE

Why do we have a separate justice system for juveniles? One reason is, of course, the basic philosophical tenet that juveniles are not as responsible for their actions as are adults.

Aside from that ancient belief, the origin of our present approach to juvenile justice can be traced back to a reform movement of the late 1800s and early 1900s. The reformers considered the urban environment with its manifold negative influences on youth to be the spawning ground of crime. Their solution was to make it illegal for kids to do all the nasty things everyone knew criminals had done when they were kids.

When prohibited by law, these naughty deeds — loitering, cursing, truancy — were known as "status offenses," because they were only illegal when committed by those of a certain status — minors.

Furthermore, reasoning that it would be best to keep kids out of adult courts, the reformers fathered an entirely new institution, the juvenile court.

As a result, today's juvenile justice system must deal with two broad categories of offenders. One category is those kids who commit actual criminal offenses, ranging in seriousness from shoplifting to murder. The second category is the status offenders, today primarily runaways, truants, and curfew violators.

101

TOO NAIVE

When we consider first just the very serious, dangerous juvenile offenders, such as those guilty of murder, rape, or robbery, it seems society has been a little too naive in dealing with them. A juvenile who commits murder will likely spend only about a year and a half in some institution.

Society has felt that heavy sentences would have little deterrent value since the assumption is that juveniles cannot adequately apply the famous "moral calculus" described by the eighteenth-century philosopher Jeremy Bentham. (Bentham's moral calculus argued that crime will be deterred if the would-be criminal views the potential punishment as too great a price to pay for the act he is contemplating.)

Yet we hear that older gang members put the guns in the hands of the younger members because they know the court will be more lenient with the young ones. And we have to wonder if these hard-core kids are not actually masters of moral calculus. After all, when a kid, after seeing an older kid hauled out of the neighborhood for some serious crime only to return a few months later, deduces that the penalty for crime is not that great, that *is* moral calculus at work.

The 15 or 16-year-old is mature enough to be strongly told that there are some things society just will not tolerate.

OVER-INSTITUTIONALIZATION

But in contrast to its treatment of the serious offender, society has for decades over-institutionalized both juveniles guilty of petty criminal offenses and status offenders.

Consider first the petty criminal — the shoplifter or the car thief, for example. More damage may ultimately result, both to the juvenile and to society, from hauling him off to some secluded reformatory rather than from risking letting him heist a few more trinkets from the local five-and-dime.

It is commonly recognized that a large percentage of

kids commit such petty crimes, to some degree or another. The vast, vast majority outgrow such behavior. For these reasons, a new school of thought has emerged which suggests that society would serve itself better if it did not take formal action against juveniles who commit petty crimes.

CONTROL THEORY

Before further discussing over-institutionalization, especially in regard to the status offender, it will be useful to briefly mention one of the most promising modern theories on the causes of crime and delinquency: control theory.

Control theory postulates that an individual's likelihood of engaging in deviant behavior is determined by the strength of his "bond" to normal society. A strong "bond" results from a high degree of *attachment* to other members of society, principally family members, and from a high *commitment* to and *involvement* in legitimate activities of society, such as education or career.

Control theory suggests that the typical juvenile offender has a weak bond with society, that is, a poor relationship with parents and probably poor performance or poor status in school. And the facts bear out what the theory suggests. A juvenile court judge commented that 70% of the kids who come into juvenile court come from broken homes.

Hans Cohn, who directs Pasadena's Rosemary Cottage, a community-based home for girls, offered the following summarization: "Essentially our youngsters are kids who have failed persistently in just about everything that they have tried, largely because their families have not given them much emotional support, because they have been shunted from place to place.... Their families have broken up, usually. They've been in foster homes. They've been in other institutions, and they've had no continuity in their lives and have not had an opportunity to settle down anywhere to develop any kind of roots."

When we institutionalize the status offender or petty juvenile criminal — when we take him out of normal

103

society — the most significant effect may be to further weaken the juvenile's already far-too-weak bond to society.

On the other hand, for some kids, especially certain status offenders, the institution may afford them their first real chance to forge a normal bond to society. This has been the case with many runaways, who, by running away, were trying to escape intolerable home conditions. Some kids get their first taste of normal life in institutions. But these are usually fairly open, community-based institutions where life for the youth is much like life on a typical block and where rules, regulations, and restrictions roughly parallel those of a normal family.

CRIME & AMERICAN VALUES

I think juvenile crime is escalating very dangerously, and it is, I think, symptomatic of a society that is morally sick....

There appears to be an erosion of the legitimacy of law in the United States. Young people today disrespect the law, disrespect the police, disrespect authority, and there's also the ethic: "I'll get what I can get." I had a young girl in my courtroom who mugged an old lady, and I questioned her afterwards about why she had done it. She said, "To get what I can get." That attitude is becoming pervasive.

Juvenile Court Judge Joseph N. Sorrentino in **The Plain Truth**, January 1977, p. 28.

Moreover, while the juvenile offender may have a weak bond to normal, legitimate society, he often has a strong bond with the quasicriminal youth subculture, such as gangs. In such a case, an institution may be the best thing that ever happened to the kid's "bonds."...

It would be best to divert the petty criminal and status offender away from juvenile court as much as possible. Then the court would have to perform only one role: that of a just, hopefully somewhat firmer-than-at-present protector of society. The court would handle, for the most part, only those juveniles who are dangerous to society or habitually criminal.

Locating Scapegoats

Instructions

The word fascism has emotional and controversial overtones. Scholars often disagree about its meaning. It conjures up images of Hitler, the swastika and Nazi horrors. During their occupation of Europe in the 1940's, the German fascists systematically killed an estimated six million Jews. They continually propagandized the outrageous lie that Jews were responsible for Germany's social ills and problems. Jews became scapegoats of irrational leaders who glorified force, violence, and the doctrines of racial supremacy. The fascists destroyed German democracy by adopting tactics of deceit and propaganda.

One of their principal propaganda weapons was the technique of scapegoating. On an individual level scapegoating involves the mental process of transferring personal blame or anger to another individual or object. Most people, for example, have kicked their table or chair as a psychological outlet for anger and frustration over a mistake or failure. On a social level, this process involves the placement of blame on entire groups of people for social problems that they have not caused. Scapegoats may be totally or only partially innocent, but they always receive more blame than can be rationally justified.

Human societies are so complex that complicated problems are often not completely understood by any citizen. Yet people always demand answers and there exists a human tendency to create imaginary and simplistic explanations for complex racial, social, economic, and political problems that defy easy understanding and solution. In times of great social turmoil, people are more prone to accept the conspiratorial ideas of those who preach hate and unreason. Conspiracy theories of history and causation represent the most dangerous form of scapegoating. This social phenomenon occurs when racial, religious, or ethnic groups are unjustly blamed for serious social problems. This blame can be expressed in terms of verbal and/or overt hatred and aggression. Although scapegoating was a major tactic of the German fascists under Hitler, it is a commonly used technique of contemporary racists and fascists in America. The following activity is designed to help you understand this technique.

"IF YOU PEOPLE HAD MORE ABORTIONS, OUR POLICE WOULD HAVE AN EASIER JOB."

Muhammed Speaks, April 20, 1973.

Part I

The above cartoon is an example of scapegoating. Examine the cartoon carefully and, with other class members, discuss why it is an example of scapegoating.

Part II

Read through the following list carefully. Some of the statements are taken from the readings in Chapter Three. Mark **S** for any statement that is an example of scapegoating. Mark **N** for any statement that is not an example of scapegoating. Mark **U** if you are undecided about any statement. Then discuss and compare your decisions with other class members.

> **S** = **An Example of Scapegoating**
> **N** = **Not an Example**
> **U** = **Undecided**

_____ 1. Our competitive economic system, which means financial failure for some, is a cause of crime.

_____ 2. Blacks are largely responsible for America's crime problems.

_____ 3. The National Rifle Association, which is against gun control legislation, can take some of the blame for crimes committed with handguns.

_____ 4. Italian Americans are responsible for organized crime in America.

_____ 5. Those who commit crimes are socially maladjusted.

_____ 6. Jews make excellent white collar criminals.

_____ 7. The disintegration of the family is a cause of crime.

_____ 8. The irresponsibility of Puerto Rican teenagers is a cause of crime.

_____ 9. Temptation by the Devil is a cause of crime.

_____10. Polish Americans, because of their lack of intelligence, are easy victims for con artists.

CHAPTER

DEALING WITH WHITE COLLAR CRIME

Viewpoints

White Collar Criminals Should Not Go To Prison

John Ehrlichman

John D. Ehrlichman, who was Richard Nixon's chief adviser for domestic affairs, was sentenced by federal Judge John Sirica to two and one-half to eight years for his role in the Watergate cover-up.

The following questions should help you examine the readings:

1. What does the author suggest as a substitute for imprisonment for white-collar criminals?
2. How does he think he should be punished for his Watergate crimes?

John Ehrlichman, ''Ehrlichman's Alternatives to Prison,'' **Minneapolis Tribune**. March 30, 1975. © 1975 by The New York Times Company. Reprinted by permission.

At my sentencing in the Watergate case, my attorney, Ira Lowe, asked not for leniency, but that I be sentenced to perform a carefully supervised term of public service as an alternative to imprisonment, to comport with the Hasidic commands of a good deed for a bad.

However, the presentation to Judge John Sirica was as much an appeal for general public debate of a vital issue as it was a plea on my behalf.

I am therefore pleased to reemphasize some of the points pressed by Lowe and others who have for many years sought alternatives to meaningless and often self-defeating imprisonment.

The issue is whether incarcerating the body of a person is better than a sentence requiring that person to spend a like term of months or years in service to other people.

It is past time for this question to be loudly asked. There are thousands of men and women in jails who are no threat to public safety; most have abilities and talents that could be put to good use. Once jailed they have little effective way to say that they could and would engage in constructive repentance if given the chance.

And most people who have not been through the corrections process have no reason to give the subject much thought. We tend not to "fix the roof if the sun is shining."

Those who do think about the prison system generally see the answer clearly. America's prisons do very little for society and less for the prisoners. Our prisons may rightly be characterized as warehouses.

There is some 15 percent of the prison population that presents a physical danger to society and must be incarcerated while we devote greater attention to this problem. Other than that, however, our prisons serve no useful purpose. The theory is to rehabilitate the offender.

But as the Oct. 15, 1973, report of the National Ad-

"I PAID TWICE OVER"

His eyes filled with tears, his voice husky as he choked back tears, the former Minnesota lawyer said he wanted to warn others that white-collar crime does not pay and those who are caught at it pay dearly.

Once a lawyer with a successful practice, he described the medium-security prison in Sandstone, Minn. as "no country club." He was sentenced to prison after he pleaded guilty to charges that he defrauded insurance companies of thousands of dollars in phony accident claims.

But being sent to jail, he said, showed a vindictiveness of the system.

"I was not a common criminal. I am not a bad man. I made a mistake and I paid twice over," he said.

Betty Washington, " 'Upper-class' Criminal Says Jail Is No Country Club," **Minneapolis Star**, November 30, 1972.

visory Commission on Criminal Justice Standards and Goals concluded: "Prisons should be repudiated as useless for any purpose other than locking away persons who are too dangerous to be allowed at large in a free society."

Even the idea of imprisonment as a deterrent to criminal conduct has little support in reality. Federal Judge Charles Richey recently observed that "the increase in our crime rate indicated that the possibility of imprisonment is not necessarily a deterrent to criminal conduct...."

In addition, the cost to the taxpayer of this warehousing of bodies can be as much as a thousand dollars per month per inmate.

Perhaps most costly and meaningless — and even arguably criminal in light of the severe need for skilled manpower to provide needed public services — is the sheer waste of talented human beings.

Columnist and author Tom Wicker has noted: "Alternatives to imprisonment are common outside the United States....Most center on providing useful training and work for the offender or keeping him in his own job if he has one while making him provide for his own dependents as well as repay anyone he may have victimized...."

Some courts in the United States have taken up the challenge. A federal judge in Phoenix recently deferred sentences for four men involved in a dairy price-fixing scheme on condition that they work on programs to feed the poor.

Also in Arizona a doctor, convicted of federal and state narcotics violations, is serving his sentence as the only doctor in the town of Tombstone, with his non-paying clientele of 4,000 residents being surrogate "probation officers."

As Lowe observed, the doctor "is not costing the taxpayers a peso, he is not rehabilitating himself by staring at the walls or writing letters to his lawyer trying to get out, and his family is not adrift to suffer."

The Pueblo Indian Council had written to Judge Sirica requesting my services. It is ironic that this has been precluded by the publicity that resulted from the raising of the question in open court. I am satisfied, however, because the larger question of alternative service and sentences has been noticed and thought about. Had it not been raised in open court this might not have been the case.

As I have already indicated to Judge Sirica, if I prove to be a successful experiment perhaps other judges would notice and grant similar opportunities to those who seem to be good prospects.

I am personally seeking to find some purpose in this whole Watergate legal process. The Watergate story is being told, written, rewritten and revised in a torrent of words. But rather than mere words, reform and regret are subjects for action now, and public service seems to

113

WHITE-COLLAR CRIME AND EVERYDAY LIFE

The phrase "white-collar crime" suggests paneled boardrooms, manicured nails, and expensively dressed executives making millions through canny stock manipulations or embezzlement.

The fact is that most economic crime is much grubbier and closer to everyday life. Repair fraud, shortweighting in food stores, product misrepresentation, and similar incidents are so common that people often don't realize they've been taken. Or if they do, they figure the money lost isn't worth the hassle to get it back.

Jack Horn, "Portrait of an Arrogant Crook," **Psychology Today**, April 1976, p. 76.

me to be the action that is called for.

Public-service sentencing is not my idea. But I associate myself with it because it is a sensible idea whose time is past due. It is not enough for only defendants and prisoners and judges and prison officials to discuss these alternatives among themselves. Thousands of people in prisons should now be seeking early release to do public service.

Enlightened legislators and other officials can now give thought, imagination and initiative to fundamental reforms and take the required action. But widespread public concern and awareness of the problem and the possibilities are indispensable.

White Collar Criminals Should Go to Prison

Roger C. Park

Roger C. Park is an Associate Professor of Law at the University of Minnesota. He attended Harvard Law School, graduating magna cum laude in 1969 and was an editor of the Harvard Law Review from 1967 to 1969.

Consider the following questions while reading:

1. Why does the author think deterrence is a good reason for imprisoning white-collar criminals?
2. How does he suggest we react to John Ehrlichman's arguments in reading 17?

Roger C. Park, "Prison Scares White-collar Criminals," **Minneapolis Tribune**, April 6, 1975.

In a column in the March 30 **Tribune**, John Ehrlichman described America's prisons as "warehouses" which do little or nothing to reform their inhabitants. His description is accurate.

Rehabilitation programs in prison have generally been dismal failures. With a few isolated exceptions, even the most ambitious programs have had no effect upon recidivism. Moreover, many prisons are designed simply to keep inmates in custody, without making any serious effort at counseling or training.

Ehrlichman argues, therefore, that offenders, who are not dangerous to society should be allowed to expiate their crimes in supervised public service. This proposal would be attractive if reformation were the only goal of criminal punishment.

In that case, a requirement that Ehrlichman render legal services to nonpaying indigents would no doubt be more beneficial both for him and for society than the 2½-to-8 year prison term imposed by Judge Sirica.

However, a more important goal of criminal punishment is deterrence — in Justice Holmes's phrase, making crime "more avoidable by others." Ehrlichman has now joined the growing group of skeptics who say that the notion of deterrence has little support in reality. This skepticism is sometimes justified, but not always.

The theory of deterrence assumes that crimes are planned rationally and that criminals weigh the gravity of punishment before committing crimes.

The available evidence suggests that many offenders commit crimes to satisfy some overriding emotional need, without really considering the consequences of their behavior.

Therefore, it is doubtful that deterrence works very well for certain types of criminals — for example, sex offenders, wife-beaters, drug users or even murderers.

The corrupt government official stands in a different posture. He is more likely to consider contingencies, weigh possibilities and calculate risks. No one doubts that Ehrlichman and his talented, intelligent colleagues did exactly that. The risks and dangers were underestimated; perhaps next time they will not be.

In the case of white-collar criminals like Ehrlichman, one frequently hears the argument that the defendant has already suffered enough by the destruction of his reputation. However, sometimes only imprisonment can serve to express the solemn moral condemnation which brands a particular activity as a "real" crime.

The need for imprisonment of white-collar criminals (at least for short terms) has been enhanced by the unfortunate proliferation of strict-liability "crimes" (for example, accidental misbranding of food products) which can be committed without any blameworthy act, and which are normally punished by fines or probation.

> It's a rare white collar offender who's what you call a first offender. It may be the first time he's apprehended, but usually the pattern that emerges is that of a person who's been cheating for an extensive period of time.

Earl J. Silbert, Washington D.C. U.S. Attorney, **Minneapolis Star**, December 1, 1976.

Crimes of perjury, obstruction of justice, official corruption and the like are not "no-fault" crimes, and they need to be stigmatized by the application of a unique sanction.

A realistic threat of imprisonment has a powerful deterrent effect upon the white-collar criminal. Marshall Clinard's study of OPA violations during World War II indicated that imprisonment, even for a short period of time, was a very frightening prospect:

"A survey of wholesale food dealers' opinions...revealed that they considered imprisonment a far more effective penalty than any other government action... some 65 percent of them make such a statement. They made remarks such as the following about jail sen-

tences: 'Jail is the only way; nobody wants to go to jail.' 'Everybody gets panicky at the thought of a jail sentence.' 'A jail sentence is dishonorable; it jeopardizes the reputation.' ''

Admittedly, the tendency to rely upon prison as a panacea for crime is deplorable. American prison sentences are generally much longer than those of other Western countries, and a sentence of 10 or 20 years can destroy a human being as surely as the death penalty.

However, the argument for shorter prison sentences

is not an argument for no prison sentences, and it is particularly not an argument for no prison sentences in the Watergate cases.

There, imprisonment will serve not only to deter (frighten) other persons who might be considering the commission of similar crimes, but to educate the public, teaching us that the obstruction of justice by persons of high position really is crime and not just political hardball, and that the law does keep its promises.

UNEQUAL SENTENCING

Should a convicted criminal be treated more leniently because he embezzled funds instead of holding up a bank? Or because he holds a relatively higher social position?

The answer obviously is "no," but it seems some judges are less severe with "white-collar" crime than with the more common variety. The thinking here is that conviction is punishment enough for a person in business whose professional reputation will be tarnished.

But such discretionary favoring of one class of criminal certainly undercuts the goal of equal justice under law.

"Coddling White-Collar Criminals," **Christian Science Monitor,** August 3, 1976.

Nixon Pardon Highlights Double Standard

Walter Mondale

Walter F. Mondale is Vice President of the United States. President Carter and Vice President Mondale won the White House race in the November election of 1976 by defeating Gerald Ford and Robert Dole. Vice President Mondale was formerly a Democratic Senator from Minnesota.

Consider the following questions while reading:

1. Why does the author think that "equal justice under law" is one of the most basic principles of our society?
2. How does the author respond to the argument that it was proper to pardon Richard Nixon because it would have been impossible for him to receive a fair trial?
3. How does Vice President Mondale think the presidential power to grant pardons should be limited?

Walter F. Mondale, **Congressional Record**, September 11, 1974.

President Ford's action on Sunday — pardoning former President Nixon — may have been an act of mercy toward Mr. Nixon. But I would like to suggest that it was an unfair, unfortunate, and unethical act toward the American people and toward our system of justice....

When he was asked — during his confirmation hearings — about the prospects for a pardon of his predecessor, Mr. Ford said: "I do not think the public would stand for it."

Mr. Ford was very right then and is very wrong now.

Not only, however, is Mr. Ford's act the ultimate coverup. It is also the ultimate injustice.

As I drive to the Capitol Building each morning, I see four words written over the portals of the Supreme Court Building across from the Capitol. Those words are "Equal Justice Under Law."

Among our most basic principles, equality before the law must rank at the very top. It is part of the due process clause of the fifth amendment binding the Federal Government. And, so there would be no mistake, was made part of the 14th amendment binding the States.

We are a nation of equality and legality.

Yet, what have the American people seen in this context over the past several months.

First, a former Attorney General enters a guilty plea to a minor offense and escapes jail entirely, after admitting lying at his own confirmation hearing about a significant matter of law enforcement.

Then, a Vice President of the United States enters a nolo contendere plea to a minor charge and escapes jail, while each of us reads 40 pages of accusations as to his illegal and immoral conduct while occupying the second highest office in the executive branch.

Now, a President of the United States resigns under pressure from his critics and his defenders after admitting lying to the American people and, possibly, being part of massive illegal activity. Yet, he too escapes significant punishment.

How do we explain to John Dean and all the others who have or will serve sentences for Watergate-related activity that Richard Nixon has a seaside view in San Clemente?

How do we explain to those who have public assistance denied to them for minor infractions that Richard Nixon is geting a $60,000 per year pension, an allowance for travel, $90,000 per year for staff salaries, and an allowance for offices?

How do we explain to the victims of burglaries, robberies, and other crimes that Richard Nixon is protected by the Secret Service?

How do we explain to the woman in Kentucky who received a lengthy jail term for stealing a pork chop to feed her family that Richard Nixon will never serve a day in jail?

How do we explain to the Vietnam deserter that Richard Nixon had unconditional amnesty — without any alternative service?

Most importantly of all, how do we explain to our children what equal justice means?

I surely do not mean to suggest that what these people did was right or that they should escape punishment. I do mean to suggest that everyone has the right to expect equal justice under our system of laws.

Theodore Roosevelt put it well when he said:

No man is above the law; every man is below it; and we need ask no man's permission when we require him to obey it.

Our system of justice must, of course, be tempered with mercy. No one takes joy from another's suffering; no one takes pleasure in a family being tortured....

I reject the notion that Mr. Nixon has suffered, in his worldview, any more than John Dean has suffered in his or than the woman in Kentucky has suffered in hers. They were destroyed — in their jobs, among their friends, and in their mental suffering — every bit as much as Mr. Nixon, if not more.

> **"I have expressed to the appropriate authorities my view that no individual holding, in the past or present, a position of major importance in the Administration should be given immunity from prosecution."**

Richard M. Nixon, April 17, 1973.

We must remember, I believe, that Mr. Nixon did not resign his Presidency; he resigned our Presidency. To the extent that he has suffered; we, too, have suffered.

Finally, I reject the notice that it would have been impossible for Richard Nixon to get a fair trial. That suggestion is an affront to the American jury system, to the American system of justice, and to the American people.

If we cannot expect equal justice in this case through the judicial system because of Mr. Ford's unfortunate act, I believe we must seriously consider whether the true national interest might not be best served by a continuation of the impeachment process.

I believe we should consider whether a House vote on impeachment followed by a Senate trial might not provide another much-needed means for fully ventilating the Watergate facts and Richard Nixon's role. At the very least, we can then prevent Richard Nixon from again holding office in this Nation.

One final measure must be given serious consideration in the wake of President Ford's action.

Although the pardon power has its rightful place in our constitutional system, it is one of the few powers that is unchecked. It is not subject to the normal pro-

I'LL TELL YOU WHY OUR CRIME RATE IS HIGH — AMERICANS ARE PLAYING 'FOLLOW THE LEADER'!"

Muhammad Speaks, April 26, 1974.

cess of checks and balances, found repeatedly throughout our Constitution.

In order to prevent abuse of that power — or use of that power in a questionable manner — I would propose a check on the pardon power. Specifically, I believe that we should consider a constitutional amendment which would allow an exercise of the Presidential pardon to be overriden by a two-thirds vote of both Houses of Congress.

Sunday's events represent a sad chapter in American history. We saw the ultimate coverup and the ultimate injustice.

As we all consider now where we go from here; how we are to put Watergate behind us in an honorable way; and how we are to prevent the results that may well follow from Sunday's events from every happening again, I believe we will do well to remember the words of former Watergate Prosecutor Archibald Cox. Although spoken in another context, they seem particularly relevent today:

> Regardless of the outcome, the value of the proceeding will depend on whether the process is so conducted that the country perceives it as a fair and legitimate measure for restoring the integrity to government.

Ford Justified
in Pardoning Nixon

Robert Griffin

Robert P. Griffin is a Republican Senator from
Michigan. He is one of the leading conservative
spokesmen in the U.S. Senate.

**The following questions should help you examine the
reading:**

1. What argument does Senator Griffin make in support of President Ford's pardon of Richard Nixon?
2. What does the senator think will be the only reason critics will have for objecting to the pardon? Do you agree?

Robert P. Griffin, **Congressional Record**, September 9, 1974.

If Presidents had been expected never to exercise the pardon power, I am sure that our Founding Fathers would not have written it into the Constitution.

Obviously they thought there would be times when considerations of mercy would justify exercise of the pardon power....

It is easy at a time like this to criticize President Ford, who has made a very difficult decision; and I have no doubt that we will hear much criticism.

This, then, was a decision that only the President of the United States is empowered to make. He has made it. It is final. It cannot be withdrawn or reversed by Congress or anyone else.

History will finally judge the actions of the President in this situation. Personally, I think he will fare very well.

It is altogether natural for one to wonder about the various considerations that must have gone into this, the most difficult decision of the new administration. President Ford had to decide: Would he move now, on the eve of action, considered almost certain, by the Special Prosecutor, Mr. Jaworski? Or would President Ford wait some indefinite, indeterminate period of time while the country resumed the agony of concern about the future of the former President?

If, after consulting with the Higher Being and his own conscience, President Ford had come to the conclusion, in his own mind, that he would grant a pardon at the end of a trial, if the former President were to be convicted, then I wonder if it is reasonable to criticize him for taking his bold and decisive action now — who can say that this does not better serve the national interest?

It is very doubtful that the former President could have gotten a speedy and a fair trial, as the Constitution guarantees to citizens accused of crime.

Furthermore, while I have no personal testimony to deliver, I have no doubt in my own mind that the condition of the health of the former President was a factor in

PARDON WAS COURAGEOUS, MAGNANIMOUS AND WISE

Having served Richard Nixon for almost nine years, this writer is anything but an objective observer. But surely time will show though the first fateful decision of the Ford presidency was controversial and costly — it was also courageous, magnanimous and wise.

How would America's interests have been served by dragging Richard Nixon back to Washington to stand trial? What benefit would have accrued to this or future generations to compensate for dragging the whole sordid Watergate mess out another year.

Some argue that, at least, the country would know the "full story" of Watergate. This is nonsense. Did anyone seriously believe that Richard Nixon,...would have taken the stand, contradicted everything he told the country and confessed at length to his involvement in the Watergate cover-up?...

Others insist that forcing Nixon to stand trial would have shown our children and the world that no man is above the law — that the law is blind and deals equally with great and small.

But this simply is not true. Presidents are above the law. They have rights and privileges no citizen enjoys. They have the power to do everything from running stoplights to ordering the army to fire on civilians to sending American soldiers into combat abroad. Unlike other citizens, we have learned, they can sit in their office and plot with impunity the assassination of foreign leaders. Presidents are not subordinate to the courts; they are the equal of the judiciary.

Patrick J. Buchanan, "Pardon in Retrospect," **Minneapolis Tribune**, September 8, 1975.

128

the decision — and the timing of the decision — by President Ford, of course, one of the most legitimate reasons for an Executive to use the pardon power is health.

Some have said that now other details about the Watergate mess may not come out. I do not think that necessarily follows, as we know, other Watergate defendants are scheduled to be tried. In the course, of those trials, additional information is likely to come out. Whether each of them can, and will, receive the fair and speedy trial guaranteed by the Constitution is a question that must be judged on a case-by-case basis.

Just as each of the others has a separate case, so the former President's case is different. It is altogether possible that we may learn more about the Watergate business now than would have been the case if the pardon had not been granted. As I understand it, possible use of the fifth amendment, for example, will no longer be available.

Now that President Ford's decision has been made, the only reasons I could imagine for any prolonged second-guessing about it would be political. I do not think the American people want the Congress to get bogged down again in the Watergate morass. This, I believe, was a major consideration in President Ford's decision. He wants the country — particularly the Congress and the administration — to focus upon and face up to the other urgent problems — like inflation — that confront our Nation and the world.

President Ford has made his decision. Whether we agree or disagree with it, we cannot change it. So, let us look forward instead of backward. Let us get on with the urgent business that really needs the attention of Congress and the country.

Understanding Stereotypes

A stereotype is an oversimplified or exaggerated description. It can apply to things or people and be favorable or unfavorable. Quite often stereotyped beliefs about racial, religious, and national groups are insulting and oversimplified. They are usually based on misinformation or lack of information.

Read through the following list carefully. Mark **S** for any statement that is an example of stereotyping. Mark **N** for any statement that is not an example of stereotyping. Mark **U** if you are undecided about any statement. Then discuss and compare your decisions with other class members.

S = Stereotype
N = Not a stereotype
U = Undecided

_____ 1. A higher percentage of American blacks than whites are criminals.

_____ 2. Mexican Americans are characteristically less ambitious and industrious than other Americans.

_____ 3. Welfare recipients are the victims of an urban, industrialized society.

_____ 4. Church members, who regularly attend services, are very unlikely to be criminals.

_____ 5. More Jews are white collar criminals than Christian Americans.

_____ 6. American Indians tend to solve problems with violence because of their ancestorial background.

_____ 7. Women are less violent than men.

_____ 8. Murderers should be punished severely.

_____ 9. Poor people often resort to crime.

_____ 10. Asian Americans have less regard for life than other Americans.

_____ 11. Italian Americans make good criminals.

_____ 12. White collar criminals should go to jail.

CHAPTER **5**

Crime &
Criminals

GUN
CONTROL
AND CRIME

The Need for Gun Control Legislation

Jonathan B. Bingham

Jonathan Bingham is serving his eleventh year in the U.S. Congress. Prior to his election in 1965, he practiced law in New York City, served in several government posts, including: an Ambassador at the United Nations under Adlai E. Stevenson.

Bring the following questions to your reading:

1. What provisions are included in Congressman Bingham's gun control bill?
2. Why does the author think a gun control bill will be passed in the near future?
3. What reasons does the author cite in support of handgun controls?
4. Why does the author want federal legislation to control gun ownership?

Jonathan B. Bingham, **Subcommittee on Crime of the House Committee on the Judiciary**, February 20, 1975.

I testify on behalf of a bill that I introduced myself on the first day of the 94th Congress, and again with 17 cosponsors. HR40:

1. Prohibits the importation, manufacture, sale, purchase, transfer, receipt, possession, or transportation of handguns or handgun ammunition, except for or by members of the Armed Forces, law enforcement officials, and as authorized by the Secretary of the Treasury, licensed importers, manufacturers, dealers, antique collectors, and pistol clubs.
2. Establishes a procedure for the licensing of pistol clubs for legitimate recreational purposes, with careful security measures for members' weapons.
3. Allows 180 days after the effective date of the Act during which any handgun owner could turn in his gun without legal liability, and receive a cash reimbursement. After this period, owners could still turn in their pistols voluntarily without risking prosecution, but would not be reimbursed.

I have been actively concerned with this issue ever since I came to Congress. But never in all the time I have been speaking out for gun control, and particularly handgun control, have I had such a sense that success is imminent. This is the Congress that can finally take action to break the grip the handgun has on America.

In a broad sense, there are only two points I want to make to the Subcommittee — first, that there is a compelling need for strict, Federal handgun control legislation; and second, that such legislation must ban the possession, as well as the manufacture and sale, of handguns if it is to be effective.

I am very pleased that these hearings are being held. Our presence here is indicative of the steadily growing national consciousness that the time has come to do something substantial about the plague of handgun violence across the nation. That consciousness is evidenced by the proliferation of editorial comments and documentary news pieces on the issue. It is evidenced also by the formation of new local and national organizations dedicated to obtaining legislative action to control handguns, and by the distinguished list of individuals and organizations who have come out for strict Federal legislation.

More and more Americans are becoming aware that there is a way to reduce the number of murders and deaths that we read about in the newspapers each day, or hear of on the TV news in the evening. They are becoming angry that Congress has not moved to do anything effective about the situation. They know that we should not tolerate 10,000 handgun murders a year. We should not tolerate all the robberies and assaults committed with handguns. We should not tolerate the accidental deaths and injuries, or the unpremeditated and often unintentional killings of friends and relatives, which happen because somewhere in the house there is a family pistol. That pistol is nearly useless for self-defense; in fact, it is six times as likely to be used against a family member as it is to be used against an intruder. It is a target for criminals. There is not one good reason for it to be there, and I propose that we remove it.)

This is not an impossible task. Most of the other nations in the civilized world have already done so, and the numbers prove the success of the approach. Tokyo, a city of 10 million, had 3 handgun murders in 1973. England and Wales, with a combined population of about 15 million, had 35 murders by firearm. Meanwhile, the United States had 13,072 gun murders, of which 10,340 were by handgun. New York City alone had over 800 handgun murders in 1973 — 23 times the gun murders in England and Wales and an incredible 266 times Tokyo's handgun murders. Our gun homicide rate is 5 times Canada's, 20 times Denmark's, 67 times Japan's, and 90 times the Netherlands'.

The desperate need for handgun control is further illustrated by this unhappy statistic; about 3 out of 4 murders are crimes of passion, in which the victim is killed by someone he or she knows, during an argument or fight. A handgun makes a point chillingly final. It probably would not be used if it were not on the mantel, or in the closet, or in a dresser drawer. No other weapon is as deadly. Death results from one in 5 gun

BAN HANDGUNS...

...before some person exercises his constitutional rights against you... or your family.

National Coalition to Ban Handguns

attacks, compared to one in 20 with a knife. We must put the family gun out of reach if we mean to end handgun death.

This bears out my second major point — only a prohibition on possession of handguns by private citizens

136

will get the job done. Proposals for registration and licensing, or for a ban on sale and transfer only, are halfway measures. A Saturday Night Special bill may eliminate cheap handguns, but cheap handguns are only a single dimension of the problem. The toll of human life taken by handguns is not related to their price or quality, or to their sale or movement. It results directly from the fact that there are about 40 million handguns in private hands. Most of these handgun owners are decent, law-abiding citizens, but their homes represent a vast warehouse for criminals. As long as those guns remain in private hands, criminals will be able to steal them, and use them to rob and murder. Our job is to close down the warehouse, not merely to stop deliveries to it or to upgrade the quality of its inventory.

I also want to emphasize briefly the need for Federal legislation. States and localities cannot do this job on their own. New York City, with one of the strictest handgun laws in the nation, is still beset with handgun problems not because the statute is weak, but because it cannot be effectively enforced in view of the absence of similar laws in nearby jurisdictions. A tough statute, uniform across the nation, is the only tool that will give law enforcement officials the means to attack the problem of handgun violence.

I recognize that even if we could pass this bill today, we wouldn't be rid of handguns tomorrow. It will take time, even with reasonable compliance and intelligent enforcement, to reduce the handgun supply and the attendant crime and death. But I know we can agree that a society free of death by handgun is a goal worthy of great striving. It is incumbent on this Congress to take the first steps down that road.

(The vast majority of Americans favor strict Federal gun control; 95% in my district. Unfortunately, this majority is all too silent, and a vocal minority have held the Congress in sway. We ought to listen to the majority we know is there.) Not a shred of evidence suggests any necessity for the possession of handguns by private citizens. We can allow it no longer. It is time to move from discussion to legislative action.

The Case Against Gun Control

Strom Thurmond

Strom Thurmond is a Republican Senator from the state of South Carolina. He has been an opponent of gun control efforts and is a spokesman for conservatives in the Congress.

As you read try to answer the following questions:

1. Why is Senator Thurmond against a national policy of gun control?
2. Why does the author think gun registration will not reduce crime?
3. What does Senator Thurmond think is the most disturbing aspect of gun control legislation?

Strom Thurmond, **Congressional Record**, January 26, 1976.

The right to keep personal firearms has been recognized in our Constitution as vital to the maintenance of individual liberty and a free society. The Founding Fathers recognized that not all men would use this fundamental right responsibly. However, they saw no need for some overreaching national government to get involved in the regulation of firearms. Our system of courts and our State and local governments would deal with specific problems as the need arose.

Unfortunately, the rise of the national bureaucracy has brought with it a different perspective on dealing with problems such as the abuse of firearms. Rather than permitting local governments to solve local problems, the bureaucratic mind conceives a universal program of regulations to be applied everywhere, whether there is a problem everywhere or not. For example, we are all alarmed at the rise in the national crime statistics. However, a rise in that national average does not mean that crime is a problem which must be dealt with in the same way everywhere. More than 20 percent of the murders committed in America are committed in New York City, and about a third of those murders are committed with firearms. But this hardly requires that we establish a national bureaucracy which will insure that the farmers and hunters of South Carolina are disarmed. Yet the centralized planner feels he must do everything himself. He must take on the responsibility himself. No one can be trusted to deal with a problem which must be solved everywhere, even if it does not exist everywhere. These administrators think that "regulation" is the proper means by which they can set things right. However, the evidence now seems to show that centralized regulation is the means by which we insure that our problem will get worse, all at great cost in tax monies and personal freedom....

Whenever the regulatory bureaucracy fail to solve the problems they were organized to solve, they ask for more resources and more power to regulate. Gun registration is a good example. In New York City, which has a strict gun registration law, somewhat fewer than 600 people have privately owned handguns which are legally registered and are not used in some form of law enforcement. Yet New York has a gun murder rate two times that of the national average to which it so greatly contributes. The New York bureaucracy cannot control guns in New York City, so it calls upon the National Government to add more regulations. But, clearly, registration is not the answer, because only law-abiding citizens register their guns. The gun murder problem in New York City is due to factors other than the existence of handguns. The State of New York has a half a million people who own handguns, but the number of registered handguns involved in crimes is extremely small.

Reprinted from **The Independent American**, October 5, 1976

Now it seems the next step in helping New York with its crime problem must be a national bureaucracy, which will regulate the 200 million guns that exist in America.

The quantity of resources which will be taken from the American people, and away from efforts to control crime, in order to nationalize the efforts to reduce New York's crime problem will be unbelievable. Depending upon which of the various programs of the antigun lobby were to be enacted into law, the costs could range as high as $5 billion a year. The average cost to taxpayers to process a gun license in New York in 1968 was $72.87 a person. Applied to the estimated 50 million gun owners, that would be around $4 billion. Add to that the price of a Federal registration system and a computer complex, probably second only in size to that

140

GUNS DO NOT CAUSE CRIME

It is a fact borne out by the FBI's own statistics that communities having the strictest regulations against guns are among the most crime-ridden in the nation. New York City, with its Sullivan Law, is a shining example....

In 1972, the state safest in number of violent crimes per 100,000 population was North Dakota, with 54.9. The safest metropolitan area was Green Bay [including Brown County] Wisconsin, with 28.6. And the place safest from murder or non-negligent manslaughter was Scranton [including Lackawanna County] Pennsylvania, with 0.4 killings per 100,000 population — as against New York City's 19.11.

⫸ Interesting, isn't it, that the places safest from violent crime in this country are states and cities in hunting areas, areas in which the incidence of private ownership of guns is higher than average, areas in which legislative restrictions against guns are far below Sullivan Law standards?

E. B. Mann, "Guns and Crime: A Look at the Record," **Field and Stream**, February 1975, p. 32.

of the Social Security Administration, and it raises the price more. The initial costs would be great and the continuing costs would be great. The American people deserve an explanation of why it would be better to spend this much money or more on the regulation of law-abiding citizens, when the same amount of money could be put into crime prevention, the courts, and the prisons.

Perhaps the most disturbing aspect of the bureaucratic approach to gun control is not that it is expensive, not that it is ineffective, but that it inevitably leads to reduction in our individual liberty and privacy, and is a danger to our system of government.

In an effort to get around constitutional guarantees, efforts are made to conjure up excuses. For example, one group has suggested that handgun ammunition be banned in interstate commerce as a hazardous substance. Is handgun ammunition more hazardous than rifle ammunition?

Legislation has been introduced which would provide a jail term and a fine for anyone who fails to turn in his handgun within 6 months of the effective date of the proposed law. Any way you look at it, this is an outrageous threat. Can you imagine the number of old firearms locked away in attics which would not be turned in?

Unjust regulation has always created a black market. Sometimes it aids the development of organized crime. Criminals become more efficient when they unite. Like the bootleggers of old, they begin as a popular resistance to pompous regulations, but eventually are almost completely replaced by organized criminals. A new problem will be created. This problem is a large criminal gun trade which will be fought with the resources now being used to stop crime in the streets.

It is appalling that some of those who advocate the abolishment of centralized recordkeeping of criminal records, and those who wish to keep the States from learning the official criminal records of criminals within their States, will at the same time advocate massive centralized dossiers on law-abiding citizens. We hear cries of protest about the arrest of persons involved in the so-called victimless crimes, and yet now they seek to create a new victimless crime.

The age-old question concerning Government regulation is raised again. Who benefits? The answer, as in so many cases, is that criminals benefit. Decent citizens and taxpayers, of course, pay the price in money and loss of freedom.

Gun Control
Will Reduce Crime

Walter E. Fauntroy

> Walter E. Fauntroy, the first person to repre-
> sent the District of Columbia in the U.S. House of
> Representatives in 100 years, was elected Dele-
> gate to the House in 1971, after the position was
> established by the Congress. He brought to his
> seat in the Congress a rich background as a civil
> rights activist and Christian minister.

Reflect on the following questions while you read:

1. What figures does the author cite to show the large
   role guns play as a cause of crime in our country?
2. Why does the author think that gun ownership by
   homeowners does not prevent crime but is instead a
   cause of crime?

Walter E. Fauntroy, **Subcommittee on Crime of the House Committee on the
Judiciary.** February 18, 1975.

As a minister and activist in the civil rights movement, I have officiated at the funerals of numerous citizens who would be alive today had we a law banning the manufacture, sale, and possession of handguns. As a minister, I have buried children who have been the innocent victims of firearms accidents because handguns were in the home. I have buried sorely missed wives and mothers, husbands and fathers whose lives were snuffed out at the tragic end of family quarrels because handguns were in the home. I have buried law-abiding citizens who were the victims of handguns used in the commission of crimes, and a very fine law enforcement officer in my church who was senselessly gunned down while handling a routine traffic violation.

I am tired of handgun funerals. In the District of Columbia, which I represent in the Congress, the leading cause of death for males under the age of forty is firearms. Last year we had a record 295 homicides in our Nation's Capital, 158 of them by handguns.

These people died, as people continue to die every day, because handguns are as accessible as they are deadly. Anyone, from the hardened criminal, to the frightened teenager committing his first crime, can easily obtain a gun, not only here in the District of Columbia, but virtually anywhere in the country. Some have estimated that there are some 200,000 handguns on the streets of the District of Columbia, and I am tired of handgun funerals.

If my remarks thus far have sounded morbid, believe me I have intended it so. I have a deep personal aversion to the private ownership of handguns that I share with the vast majority of American citizens today.

Lest you think that handgun deaths are just a problem to me personally or unique to the District Columbia, let me remind you that every city in the United States has this problem.

Guns are responsible for an average of sixty-nine deaths each day in America. Of the 25,000 gun deaths occurring each year, 12,000 are homicides, 10,000 are suicides, and 3,000 are accidents. One out of every hundred deaths in the United States is caused by a gun. Forty percent of the victims are 19 years old or less. In addition, some 200,000 people are wounded by firearms

GUNS DON'T DIE...

PEOPLE DO!

MARLETTE IN THE CHARLOTTE OBSERVER

each year, resulting in paralyzation, sterilization, dismemberment, blindness, deafness, and other disabling effects.

In 1972, 54 percent of all murders committed were carried out by handguns.

Between 1969 and 1974, armed robbery increased 75 percent, and both aggravated assault and gun murder were up 50 percent. Our population did not increase in such vast proportions.

Most murders are committed by previously law-abiding citizens where the killer and victim are acquainted — approximately 25 percent occur within families. These are murders which could well have been prevented by gun control.

The fact is that guns in the home do not prevent lawlessness, violence and death; they cause it. For every intruder stopped by a home-owner with a gun, there are four accidents in the home. Close to 3,000 accidental deaths are caused by firearms each year. One fourth of the victims are under 14 years old.

Handguns are involved in a majority of all police killings. During the period of 1964-73, firearms were used by felons to commit 95 percent of the police killings. During this period, 858 law enforcement officers were slain: 613 were killed with handguns, 104 with rifles, 101 with shotguns, the remaining forty were killed with weapons other than guns.

HANDGUNS ARE FOR ONE THING

Handguns are practical for only one thing — killing people. And they do. Approximately 32,000 Americans died by the gun in 1974 [the last year for which there are figures] — 15,000 murders, 14,000 suicides, 3,000 accidents. Almost 80% of gun murders are committed with handguns. And nearly three murders out of four are "crimes of passion" — murders where the victim is a family member, friend or neighbor. Most of these murders take place when a desperate individual has access to a handgun in a moment of rage or insanity; if no handgun were available, most of these murders simply would not happen.

National Coalition to Ban Handguns

The three Federal law enforcement officers killed in 1973 were killed by the use of handguns.

It is impossible to measure the full impact of handguns in homicide statistics alone. There are countless rapes, robberies, assaults carried out with handguns. A gun gives the criminal the God-like power of life and death over ordinary citizens. We must get guns out of

146

the hands of criminals, and my legislation will set the framework for doing it.

The number of handguns in the United States is estimated as high as 40 million — or about one gun for every 5 persons. In recent years there has been a great increase in the number of such weapons. The incredible proliferation of firearms in the United States, however, is not part of a world-wide trend. The total number of gun deaths in all other free nations is exceeded by the number of gun deaths in the United States alone.

With proper gun control laws, the gun death rates of the United States could someday favorably compare with those of the rest of the world.

State and local laws cannot be effective in controlling this menace. There is demonstrated need for immediate strong and comprehensive national legislation.

Gun Control Does Not Reduce Crime

National Rifle Association

> The following statement was testimony given before the Subcommitte on Crime of the House Committee on the Judiciary on October 1, 1975 by Harlan B. Carter. Mr. Carter was then serving as Executive Director of the Institute for Legislative Action of the National Rifle Association.

Consider the following questions while reading:

1. Why does the NRA claim that restrictive gun laws do not reduce crime?
2. What does the NRA think might happen if a federal gun control law is enacted?

Harlan B. Carter, **Subcommittee on Crime of the House Committee on the Judiciary**, February 18, 1975.

Law abiding people, and particularly gun owners, are tired of being blamed for crime. They are sick of being harassed with federal bureaucracy and having their freedom progressively and incessantly chipped away because of the inability or unwillingness of their government officials to deal with those responsible for crime, namely, criminals.

In 1973, 20 per cent of all the murders in the nation occurred in four cities: Chicago, Detroit, New York City and Washington, D.C. It is highly illuminating that each of those four cities has extremely restrictive gun laws — among the most extreme gun control laws in the nation.

A small percentage of the population is causing most of the crime, and the existence of firearms is not affecting the crime rates in the areas where those laws exist.

We've all heard a great deal of talk about how states with strict gun laws are being thwarted by people who are gun running from states where the gun laws are not as strict. The officials who are charged with enforcement of the current federal laws describe in extreme detail where these guns come from and the route by which they get to their destinations. What I have not heard a great deal about — and it truly mystifies me — is why aren't these people who buy from them, why aren't they in jail? Why is the Justice Department — which is so eager to impose additional restrictions on the law-abiding — so unwilling to prosecute flagrant violations of existing firearms laws?

It is said that New York and Detroit have high crime rates because of guns from Ohio and South Carolina. How can that be true when Ohio and South Carolina, with all their guns still have lower crime rates — a lower murder rate — than New York or Michigan? Wouldn't one reasonably assume something besides guns is at the root of the matter?

It is already a violation of federal law, with very severe penalties up to five years in prison, for moving firearms between the states, except between licensed dealers. It just simply seems outrageous that new gun laws would be sought upon such a fallacious pretext.

Strait Jacket Would Be on the Wrong Guy

Why haven't all the gun laws that we already have — federal, state and local — which make it impossible for a criminal to lawfully have a gun in the first place, prevented street crime in our cities?

In an attempt to justify taking firearms out of the hands of the law-abiding, the proponents of some of the bills before you have contended that since most murders are between relatives and persons acquainted with one another that most murderers are therefore law-abiding citizens. But that is nonsense. Criminals also have relatives and acquaintances. Junkies know their pushers; pimps know their prostitutes.

An analysis of 970 murders committed in Chicago during 1974 revealed that over 60% of the murderers had prior criminal records and nearly one-half of their victims had a prior criminal record. Clearly, murderers

150

are not average hard-working, tax-paying, law-abiding citizens.

But for reasons nobody has been able to explain — at least to my satisfaction — many of the men and women in control of our institutions seem unable to grasp the fact that there are mindless, cold-blooded, and evil people who daily commit unspeakable violence against which our institutions fail to protect the vast majority of innocent citizens who are victimized. They simply refuse to recognize that certain criminals must be removed from society for the protection of society.

These same people in the media, in the Congress, in the courts seem to blame crime on everything in our society except the criminal and want to punish anyone and anything except the criminals.

There are very few victims of brutal criminality who wonder or even care about the socio-economic conditions that may or may not have motivated their attacker. The surviving victims of crime know only that they have been robbed, or beaten, or stabbed, or mugged, raped or shot. They have suffered. And under our system of justice — or at least as it was designed — the criminal who directly caused that suffering is supposed to pay the consequences. But somehow, it doesn't work that way any more.

There is a very clear breakdown in our criminal justice system, when the Attorney General of the United States tells us that we have only a four per cent conviction rate of serious felonies and even fewer go to jail.

I do not believe that it's possible to take enough guns away from criminals to ensure the safety of a disarmed public. But if the President is right — if most crime is attributable to a relatively small number of criminals, we can take them — the criminals — out of circulation.

It astonishes me that those who are most concerned about the civil liberties of our citizens should attack the liberties of law-abiding citizens who own guns.

It amazes me that those who created the Privacy Act

151

and who denounce any plan for centralized files upon our citizens would now demand a centralized file upon citizens who happen to be gun owners. We oppose all dossiers on law-abiding citizens!

It appalls me that those who demand an end to so-called victimless crimes would attempt to create a new victimless crime by prosecuting a person who simply owns a handgun and had committed no other offense.

Finally, it astounds me that we would alienate a sizeable percentage of our citizens, who are firmly convinced that they have a basic, fundamental right to possess a firearm for defense of themselves and their families. It is sad to say, but I believe that it is undeniably true, that if this body were to declare all firearms contraband, it would be inviting civil disobedience.

In the face of such a mountain of evidence that gun laws have failed to reduce crime, how can anyone reasonably assume that yet another gun law will reduce crime?

We question the assumptions upon which these three proposals, and all similar measures, are based. We have yet to see any evidence that the ideas which they incorporate have worked. We have seen ample evidence that they do not.

Cause and Effect Relationships

This discussion exercise provides practice in the skill of analyzing cause and effect relationships. Causes of human conflict and social problems are usually very complex. The following statements indicate possible causes of crime. Rank them by assigning the number (1) to the most important cause, number (2) to the second most important, and so on until the ranking is finished. Omit. any statements you feel are not causative factors. Add any causes you think have been left out. Then discuss and compare your decisions with other class members.

_____ 1. decline of religion

_____ 2. poverty

_____ 3. a permissive society

_____ 4. bad parents

_____ 5. corrupt public officials

_____ 6. unemployment

_____ 7. drugs

_____ 8. uncertain punishment for crime

_____ 9. ineffective schools

_____ 10. dehumanizing prisons

_____ 11. organized crime

_____ 12. a rip-off mentality

153

SELECTED PERIODICAL BIBLIOGRAPHY

Because most school libraries have a rather limited selection of books on crime, the editors have compiled a bibliography of helpful and recent periodical articles. Most school libraries have back issues of periodicals for at least a few years, and it is hoped that the following entries will be of some help to the student who wants to study crime and criminals in more depth.

CRIME AND ITS CAUSES

Annals
Crime and Justice in America, January 1976 (special issue).

Connie Bruck
Women Against the Law, **Human Behavior** December 1975, p. 25.

Christianity & Crisis
Rethinking Criminal Justice, February 17, 1975 (special issue).

Christianity Today
Coping With Crime, June 6, 1975, p. 30.

Current History
Criminal Justice In America, June 1976 (special issue).

Reforming the Criminal Justice System, July/ August 1976 (special issue).

Edward H. Levi
The Attorney General Speaks Out, **U.S. News & World Report**, June 30, 1975, p. 30.

Donald T. Lunde
Our Murder Boom, **Psychology Today**, July 1975, p. 35.

Patrick V. Murphy
Our Disgraceful System of Combating Crime, **Reader's Digest**, February 1974, p. 169.

New Republic
Of Two Minds About Crime, May 1, 1975, p. 3.

Skeptic
November/December 1974 (special issue on crime).

Society
Crime and Punishment, July/August 1974 (special issue).

Time
The Crime Wave, June 30, 1975, p. 10.

Lou Torok
A Convict Looks at Crime and Criminals, **America**, January 13, 1973, p. 10.

U.S. News & World Report
War On Crime, September 29, 1975, p. 19.

J. P. Widgery — *How Britain Handles Crime: Dispose of Cases Quickly*, **U.S. News & World Report**, January 27, 1975, p. 45.

James Q. Wilson — *Lock 'Em Up And Other Thoughts On Crime*, **New York Times Magazine**, March 9, 1975, p. 11.

DEALING WITH CRIMINALS

Business Week — *Crime: A Case For More Punishment*, September 15, 1975, p. 92.

Sol Chanels — *Prisoners Can Be Rehabilitated Now*, **Psychology Today**, October 1976, p. 129.

A. Dershorvitz — *Let the Punishment Fit the Crime*, **New York Times Magazine**, December 28, 1975, p. 7.

Amitai Etzioni — *The Social Base of Vigilantism*, **Human Behavior**, March 1976, p. 14.

M. McLaughlin — *Sentences That Make Sense*, **McCalls**, February 1975, p. 40.

Robert Mack — *Certainty of Punishment Is Best Deterrent To Crime*, **U.S. News & World Report**, May 10, 1976, p. 41.

Time — *Crime and Punishment*, April 26, 1974, p. 82.

U.S. News & World Report — *A War On Career Criminals Starts to Show Results*, November 22, 1976, p. 73.

Big Change In Prisons, Punish — Not Reform, August 25, 1975, p. 21.

DEALING WITH JUVENILE OFFENDERS

C. Holden — *Massachusetts Juvenile Justice: De-Institutionization On Trial*, **Science**, April 30, 1976. p. 447.

Jack Horn — *Juvenile Status Offender — Neither Fish Nor Fowl*, **Psychology Today**, August 1975, p. 31.

Patrice Horn — *Family Therapy — A Quick Fix For Juvenile Delinquency*, **Psychology Today**, March 1975, p. 80.

Intellect — *Delinquency Patterns Among Adolescents*, December 1974, p. 144.

New Program to Reduce Delinquency, July 1975, p. 9.

P. Moore — *Small Towns Breed Delinquents Too*, **Psychology Today**, December 1974, p. 40.

Ted Morgan	*They Think "I Can Kill Because I'm 14,"* **New York Times Magazine**, January 19, 1975. p. 9.
Newsweek	*Children and the Law*, September 8, 1975, p. 66.
J. D. Truby	*Fighting Juvenile Crime: Volunteers in Probation*, **Parents Magazine**, July 1975, p. 44.
U.S. News & World Report	*Coming: Tougher Approach to Juvenile Violence*, June 7, 1976, p. 65.

DEALING WITH WHITE COLLAR CRIME

Murry Teigh Bloom	*Why Coddle White Collar Criminals?* **Reader's Digest**, January 1977, p. 132.
William F. Buckley, Jr.	*Let Him Go*, **National Review**, August 30, 1975, p. 996.
Christian Century	*Everybody's Doing It?* March 24, 1976, p. 278.
Jack Horn	*Portrait of An Arrogant Crook*, **Psychology Today**, April 1976, p. 76.
G.C. Lodge & F.T. Allen	*Are Payoffs Abroad Ever Justified?* **U.S. News & World Report**, April 12, 1976, p. 35.
The Nation	*The Corporate Crime Wave*, September 6, 1975, p. 164.
C.W. Parker	*Bribery In Foreign Lands*, **Vital Speeches**, February 15, 1976, p. 281.
L. Smith	*Is Business Soft On Crime?* **Duns Review**, August 1976, p. 49.

GUN CONTROL AND CRIME

John M. Ashbrook	*Against Comprehensive Gun Control*, **Current History**, July 1976, p. 23.
James Billington	*The Gun Within*, **Newsweek**, October 6, 1975, p. 13.
Commonweal	*Taming Our Violence*, October 10, 1975, p. 451.
Congressional Digest	*Controversy Over Proposed Federal Handgun Control*, December 1975 (special issue on gun control legislation).
Louis Gasper	*Pistols, Registration and Confiscation*, **New Guard**, July/August 1972, p. 13.
Barry Goldwater	*Why Gun-Control Laws Don't Work*, **Reader's Digest**, December 1975, p. 183.

M.F. Harvey | *They Have Gun Controls in England*, **National Review**, September 15, 1972, p. 1007.

Edward M. Kennedy | *Need For Gun Control Legislation*, **Current History**, July 1976, p. 26.

E.B. Mann | *By Their Words You Shall Know Them*, **Field and Stream**, August 1975, p. 30.

Guns and Crime: A Look At the Record, **Field and Stream**, February 1975, p. 32.

Martin E. Marty | *It Ain't Necessarily So*, **Field and Stream**, July 1975, p. 107.

Thomas H. Middleton | *Uncivil Religion*, **Christian Century**, June 9, 1976, p. 583.

How To Win Public Opinion Polls, **Saturday Review**, August 23, 1975, p. 61.

The Nation | *Gunning For Trouble*, September 27, 1975, p. 260.

Killer Society, September 13, 1975, p. 196.

Alan E. Sherman | *Gun Legislation: Who Does It Really Protect?* **Pro/Con Magazine**, August 1970.

U.S. News & World Report | *How One State's Gun-Control Law Is Working*, August 30, 1976, p. 35.

Paul J. Weber | *The National Rifle Association: Public Enemy Number 2*, **Christian Century**, October 16, 1974, p. 958.

Violence Stalks the Land, **America**, December 29, 1973, p. 501.

James D. Wright | *The Demography of Gun Control*, **The Nation**, September 20, 1975, p. 240.

meet
the editors

Gary E. McCuen received his A.B. degree in history from Ripon College. He also has an M.S.T. degree in history from Wisconsin State University in Eau Claire, Wisconsin. He has taught social studies at the high school level and is currently working on additional volumes for the Opposing Viewpoints Series.

DAVID L. BENDER is a history graduate from the University of Minnesota. He also has an M.A. in government from St. Mary's University in San Antonio, Texas. He has taught social problems at the high school level and is currently working on additional volumes for the Opposing Viewpoints Series.